Violence Goes to School

John Nicoletti, Ph.D.
and
Sally Spencer–Thomas, Psy.D.

National Educational Service

Copyright © 2002 by National Educational Service
304 West Kirkwood Avenue; Suite 2
Bloomington, IN 47404
(800) 733-6786 (toll free) / (812) 336-7700
FAX: (812) 336-7790
www.nesonline.com

Cover Design by Grannan Graphic Design, Ltd.
Text Design and Composition by TG Design Group

Printed in the United States of America

ISBN: 1-879639-88-2

Contributors

Nikki Aggers

Mary Atwater

Evan Axelrod

Kym Baum

Lottie Flater

Kari Haska

Kathryn Porter

Debra Tasci

Kelly Zinna

Acknowledgements

We would like to thank the following people and agencies for their help in preparing and reviewing this book and for their support of the authors:

Lynn Lower

Bill Porter

Jon DeStefano

Regis University—Dayton Memorial Library

U.S. Secret Service

Federal Bureau of Investigation

Colorado Law Enforcement Agencies

Denver Metro School Districts

Jerene Anderson and Susan Richardson

Lottie Flater and Randy Thomas

We dedicate this book
to all those people who are working toward
preventing and interrupting school violence.

Table of Contents

About the Authors

John Nicoletti, Ph.D., is the cofounder of Nicoletti–Flater Associates with his spouse, Lottie Flater, and has been a police psychologist in the Denver metro area for more than 25 years. In the years since the Columbine tragedy, Dr. Nicoletti has been sought internationally for his expertise in school violence prevention. He was an invited speaker at the 10th World Conference in Disaster Management (June 2000, Toronto, Ontario, Canada) and was a keynote speaker at the 2001 National Students Assistance Conference (April 2001, Orlando, Florida). Dr. Nicoletti was also asked by the Columbine Review Commission to testify numerous times and is cited often in *The Report of Governor Bill Owens' Columbine Review Commission* (May 2001).

Over the last 10 years, the Nicoletti–Flater private practice has expanded into the field of violence assessment and violence prevention. After years of working with national corporations and government agencies such as the United States Postal Service, United Airlines, NASA, Johns Manville, and the U.S. Department of Energy, Dr. Nicoletti established himself as a national expert in workplace violence. In 1993, he cowrote and published *Violence Goes to Work* (since reprinted four times), a very well received prevention manual for employers, and *Violence Goes to College: The Authoritative Guide to Prevention and Intervention.*

Dr. Nicoletti has conducted hundreds of workshops, training seminars, and consultations across the country. He has been featured on CBS Evening News with Dan Rather ("Tragedy in Littleton: Those Who Went Inside" [April 26, 1999] and "Columbine Survivor Struggles with Memories Day by Day" [April 20, 2000]); NBC Nightly News with Tom

Brokaw ("Workplace Violence," February 5, 2001); Fox News ("Workplace Violence," December 22, 1998); Denver's Channel 2 (KWGN); and Channel 9 News (KUSA), sharing his expertise on violence-related topics. He has also been quoted in *The Washington Post, The Philadelphia Inquirer, The Denver Post,* and *The Rocky Mountain News.*

Dr. Nicoletti has received many awards for his distinguished contributions to the field of psychology. Most notably, in 1996 the Colorado Psychological Association awarded him the E. Ellis Graham award and in 1998 the American Psychological Association awarded him the Karl F. Heiser Presidential Award for advocacy on behalf of professional psychology. Recently, the House of Representatives of Pennsylvania recognized him for his "vital and meaningful work in helping our country's citizens overcome the horror and tragedy of violence...."

In 1972, Dr. Nicoletti received his Ph.D. in Counseling Psychology from Colorado State University. He has completed specialized training from the FBI and the DEA in such areas as criminal profiling and tracking, the analysis of threats and violence, and trauma intervention techniques. He is a member of the Association of Threat Assessment Professionals and the International Association of Chiefs of Police. He has one daughter who is an elementary school teacher.

Sally Spencer-Thomas, Psy.D., received her doctorate in clinical psychology from the University of Denver in 1995. For almost a decade, she has worked in the roles of health psychologist, therapist, program developer, and violence prevention consultant in her work with Regis University and Nicoletti-Flater Associates.

As an employee of the Denver Police Department, she served as a Victim Advocate by counseling and providing resources for families in crisis. Dr. Spencer-Thomas received specialized training in Post-Traumatic Stress

Disorder (PTSD) from the Boston VA Medical Center. Drs. Nicoletti and Spencer–Thomas have coauthored numerous violence prevention publications, including

- *Survival-Oriented Kids in a Violent World: A Skills Training Manual for Parents and Other Protectors* (Nicoletti–Flater Associates, 1998)

- *Violence Goes to College: The Authoritative Guide to Prevention and Intervention* (Charles C. Thomas, 2001)

- "A Cognitive Social Processing Model for Assessing and Treating Domestic Violence and Stalking by Law Enforcement Officers," in Federal Bureau of Investigation, *Domestic Violence by Police Officers* (U.S. Department of Justice, 2000).

- "Contamination of Cops: Police Response to Civilian Suicide," in Federal Bureau of Investigation, *Suicide and Law Enforcement.* (U.S. Department of Justice, 2001).

Dr. Spencer–Thomas was also honored to present to the FBI Academy (Quantico, Virginia) on suicide and law enforcement in the fall of 1999.

Additionally, Dr. Spencer–Thomas runs the Behavioral Health Program at Regis University, focusing on violence prevention, substance abuse, and other health issues. She has presented workshops on college violence to campus professionals around the country. Currently, she is serving as the Area 3 Consultant of the BACCHUS and GAMMA Peer Education Network, and has overseen Regis's award winning peer education program since 1995. She also is the mother of Nicholas and Tanner.

Preface

We at Nicoletti–Flater Associates were on the scene within 45 minutes of the first shots fired at Columbine High School on April 20, 1999, offering aid to families and public safety officers at the command center. That evening we helped victims' families at nearby Leawood Elementary School. During the days and weeks that followed, we conducted debriefings for many affected groups in the Denver metro area, reaching law enforcement personnel, SWAT team members, bomb squads, investigators, and victim–assistance units. We have counseled victims, families, police officers, and others who were emotionally affected by the events of that day.

However, the tragedy at Columbine was not our first encounter with this form of violence. As a police psychology firm with a national reputation in violence prevention and intervention, specifically violence in the workplace, we have been closely watching the unfolding of schoolyard events since the early 1990s. We perceived and interpreted these incidents in a way that was familiar to us yet different from the views of our mental health colleagues and those of school personnel. We immediately saw a dramatic and striking parallel between the violence occurring in the schools and a phenomenon we know so well, workplace violence.

Others did not initially make the connection. Parents, teachers, and even mental health experts insisted these events were simply an extension of the same random acts of violence that have been perpetrated by school kids since the beginning of organized schooling. Their solutions were essentially reruns of old advice: encourage parents to listen to their children, identify and treat mental health problems earlier, give kids appropriate supervision, etc. We consider all these suggestions to be worthwhile, but contend that they are insufficient to counter this new and very different problem.

The more information we gathered about the school shootings, the more convinced we became that the dynamics were very similar to those of workplace violence. We began comparing the two phenomena so often that we coined the hybrid term *schoolplace violence* to describe this new and frightening entity. Many were unnerved by the likening of these adult crimes with adult motivations to acts committed by children and adolescents, and our ideas were often dismissed. However, we continued to collect evidence and to document the similarities and differences between the two types of violence, noting many variables, including types of threats made, precipitating factors, and post-incident behaviors.

Combining the knowledge gained at Columbine with more than a decade of learning in the workplace, we have arrived at a model of prevention and intervention that we have been able to share in workshops and training seminars across the nation. John Nicoletti was asked on more than one occasion to testify before the Columbine Review Commission, and the prevention and intervention information collected here has already been touted as a model program in Colorado Governor Bill Owens's report on the Commission's findings. We are pleased to be able to offer our findings in book form at last. For the past several years we have been able to give selected schools real-life solutions that offer immediate empowerment in the face of impending violence. With this book we aim to make these solutions available to all.

Note to the reader: All information provided herein is general in nature and designed to serve as a guide to understanding. These materials are not to be construed as the rendering of legal or management advice. If the reader has a specific need or problem, the services of a competent professional should be sought to address the particular situation. For more information or consultation, contact Nicoletti-Flater Associates at 3900 South Wadsworth Boulevard, Suite 480, Lakewood, CO 80433; 303-989-1617; www.n-fa.com.

Introduction

Who Should Read This Book?

Everyone concerned with school violence should read this book—school administrators, school resource officers, teachers, and those who wish to develop response and prevention plans to handle threats and violence in schools. This book is meant for them. But parents and other protectors may also wish to read this book, which includes information that may help them understand and deal with the disturbing phenomenon of school violence—even if they are not directly affected. While many resources purport to help prevent and deter aggression and violence in children, the advice offered usually covers familiar suggestions for improved parenting and mental health services. This manual adds to that body of work a focus on the immediate: immediate response, immediate empowerment of both adults and young people, and immediate courses of action to be taken before, during, and after a threatened or actual violent event.

The material provided in this guide is designed for those who already recognize the extensive damage school violence causes and are searching for ways to address this problem before another incident occurs. The book offers step-by-step advice about early identification of problems, intervention and prevention techniques, and containment procedures that can reduce the risk of school violence. Our emphasis is on "in the moment" direction—practical suggestions about how to prepare for and respond to schoolplace violence as defined in this book. Because each school setting is unique, responsible protectors should consult with a professional to address the specifics of serious situations.

What This Book Is, and What It Is Not

The nature, scope, and levels of school violence are broad. Educational institutions are continually challenged to devise ways to meet and defuse each type of violence encountered on school grounds. Physical altercations, gang violence, vandalism, and spree shootings are just a few of the kinds of violence operating in schools today. This guide focuses on a specific type of violence that parallels the dynamics of adult workplace violence—the spree-shooting type we have identified as schoolplace violence. Gang activity, bullying, and other forms of school violence are beyond the scope of the book, and we have listed additional resources on pages 207–210 to help schools with these types of problems.

In this book, we do not spend a great deal of time focusing on reasons why school shootings are happening. There are many resources that explore the broad societal, biological, and cultural influences at work in youth violence. In this book, we focus primarily on the "now what."

We believe the dynamics of schoolplace violence are reasonably identifiable, and that prevention is therefore possible. This guide outlines proactive measures that, when undertaken by school personnel, will help reduce the possibility of this type of tragedy occurring. Long-term pre-vention strategies that deal with the teaching of prosocial values, with diversity appreciation, anger and conflict management, or bullying pre-vention are also beyond the scope of this book. Longitudinal studies measuring the impact of these types of programs have yielded mixed results (Elliott, Hamburg, & Williams, 1998; Gottfredson, Fink, Skroban, & Gottfredson, 1997; Gottfredson, Gottfredson, Czeh, Cantor, Crosse, & Hantman, 2000). While most schools have violence prevention programs, the programs tend to be put together in a piecemeal fashion. Program content that has shown promising results includes teaching develop-mentally appropriate skills for living according to nonviolent norms. These skills include social competence, anger management, impulse con-trol, and empathy. Schools that have been successful in violence reduc-tion have also implemented effective classroom behavior management and have promoted school bonding.

Perhaps even more important than the content of these programs is the process through which they are developed. Effective programs go beyond one-shot presentations for children. Rather, high quality programs are planned, comprehensive, and ongoing. They are supported by the principal, engage parents, train teachers and support staff, and involve the

Part I

Schoolplace Violence Overview

Chapter One

Schoolplace Violence: Fad or Trend?

What Is Happening With Youth Violence?

In the last few years, our country's leading experts and respected agencies have attempted to analyze the trends in youth violence and have generated impressive reports. The U.S. Department of Education, the Surgeon General, the Centers for Disease Control, and others have put tremendous resources toward trying to understand patterns in youth violence.

In October 2000, the U.S. Department of Education reported that in the years 1997 and 1998, students 12 to 18 years of age were victims of more than 2.7 million crimes at school. Of those, 253,000 were serious violent crimes, including rape, sexual assault, robbery, and aggravated assault.

The same report reveals that over a 1–year period, 15% of students in grades 9 through 12 reported having been in a physical fight on school property. One national study found that almost one in five students reported being threatened with a beating, with middle school students experiencing this more frequently than high school students (Gottfredson, Gottfredson, Czeh, et al., 2000). According to the Center for the Study and Prevention of Violence (CSPV), 20% of high school students reported carrying a weapon at least once in the month preceding the National Youth Risk Behavior Survey (CSPV, 1999c).

These statistics are clearly of concern. People want to know: Is youth violence increasing or decreasing? The answer to that question is complicated. It depends on who you ask, how you measure the violence, and what time span you are looking at.

Is Youth Violence Decreasing?

The U.S. Surgeon General's Report (2001b) states that there are signs that youth violence is on the decline. However, the percentage of adolescents involved in violent behavior continues to be disturbingly high. Four key indicators inform us about the current state of youth violence: arrest records, victimization data, hospital emergency room records, and confidential youth self-reports. According to the Surgeon General's report, there was an unprecedented surge of violence between 1983 and 1993. Events in this time period have been dubbed an "epidemic of youth violence." Since 1993, the first three indicators show a decline in youth violence. The fourth indicator, youth self-reports, remains constant at the same alarming level as in 1993. The report attributes the rise and fall of the first three indicators to the accessibility of firearms.

According to the journal *Criminal Justice Ethics* (cited in Cloud, 2001), more than 99.99% of public schools have never had a homicide, and homicide rates on school campuses have dropped significantly—from 54 during the 1992–1993 school year to 16 during the 1999–2000 school year. The Centers for Disease Control (CDC) concurs that homicide rates for young males began to decline in 1994 and dropped 34% between 1993 and 1997 (CDC, 2000). Nevertheless, all sources agree that these rates remain unacceptably high.

The Surgeon General reports that youth homicide, robbery, and rape arrest rates in 1999 were lower than 1983 levels (U.S. Surgeon General, 2001b). The U.S. Department of Education (2000) reports that the rate of serious violent crime (defined as rape, sexual assault, robbery, and aggravated assault) remained fairly stable from 1992 to 1998. Both sources agree that fewer students are carrying guns.

The problem with much of the data indicating a decline in youth violence is the dependence on arrest records. Arrest records under-estimate youth violence. Most youth involved in violent crimes are never arrested (Elliot, 1989; Loeber & Farrington, 1998). Research has shown that most crimes committed by our country's youth are not reported and therefore are not part of the larger picture of youth violence. Self-reports by youth provide us with a way to measure violent behavior that has not been reported to the police or tracked by emergency room records. Youth self-reports tell quite a different story.

Is Youth Violence Increasing?

In contradiction to the data provided by arrest records, victimization data, and emergency room records, the youth in this country are telling us that the proportion of youth who acknowledged committing serious and potentially lethal acts of physical violence has remained constant since the peak of the epidemic of youth violence.

According to the U.S. Surgeon General (2001b), the 1990s, when compared to any previous decade, had at least 10 times as many youths reporting that they had taken part in some form of violent behavior that potentially could have seriously injured or killed another human. Furthermore, from 1993 to 1997, the percentage of students in grades 9 through 12 who reported having been threatened or injured by a weapon on school grounds remained constant. The number of students reporting having been in a physical fight on school grounds also held constant during this time.

Other means of assessing youth violence are homicide rates and teachers' reports. The Center for the Study and Prevention of Violence (CSPV) reports that homicide rates among adolescents have increased dramatically in the last decade—much faster than rates of nonfatal assaultive behavior (CSPV, 1999a). This increase is largely due to homicides involving firearms. The CSPV further reports that suicide rates among adolescents have more than tripled since the early 1950s, and the increase in this rate is also largely attributable to the use of firearms.

The Center for the Prevention of School Violence (1999) cites the following statistics:

- The U.S. Department of Education's 1999 *Annual Report on School Safety* stated that although fewer school-associated violent deaths have occurred in recent years, the total number of multiple-victim homicide events has increased.

- The 1999 Metropolitan Life Survey of the American Teacher reported that 1 in 6 teachers states that he or she has been the victim of violence in or around school. This percentage increased from 1 in 9 teachers 5 years before.

What Is the Problem With These Questions?

The Dangers of Over-Generalizing

When we look at patterns in such a broad concept as "youth violence," we run the risk of generalizing useful trends right out of existence. Youth violence studies tend to lump several different forms of violence—gang violence, bullying, theft, sexual assault, and school shootings—into a single undifferentiated group. But this is a mistake because each of these forms of violence has different objectives and outcomes. Youth violence that happens on school grounds is different from youth violence that happens in the home or in the community. We get a clearer picture of patterns in youth violence when we look at different subsets separately.

Violence Is Like a Virus

Violence is like a virus with many different strains. Motives, perpetrator characteristics, victims, and effects are diverse, and these features of violence mutate, like a virus, when exposed to different hosting environments. Understanding violence in terms of its similarities to a virus can help prevention and intervention efforts. Violence is not static. Each time the virus mutates, those who seek to prevent it fall behind.

Too often, different strains of violence are lumped together when people attempt to develop prevention strategies. People assume that violence does not mutate. Many assume that similar forms of violence have the same impact in different environments. Or they assume that different forms of violence impact the same environment in the same way. For instance, in the aftermath of the tragedy at Columbine, dozens of national "violence summits" were convened in an attempt to find solutions to school violence. At these meetings hundreds of experts and concerned protectors gathered to discuss a multitude of violence issues, including gang violence, bullying, hate crimes, sexual abuse, and more.

Frequently, attendees left feeling increased confusion rather than clarity. Many sought the magical elixir—the one cure-all—and found that it did not exist.

A prevention strategy may be effective with a particular type of violence in a particular setting, but that tactic may lose its potency when the strain of violence moves to a different hosting environment or to a different population. For example, drug-related violence on the street presents a different set of challenges than when it spills over into school grounds. For one thing, there are many more potential victims in a congested school setting. The violence takes different paths on the street than in the schoolyard. The impact of violence changes when victims are targeted alone at night or in a crowded school during the day. Thus, different settings require individually tailored interventions.

We must begin to look at the different strains of youth violence separately. Each eruption calls for unique solutions. In this book we address a rare but exceptionally terrifying form of youth violence that has recently dominated the thinking of parents, teachers, school officials, and students: the schoolplace violence epitomized in most Americans' minds by the events at Columbine High School in April 1999.

Perception Is Reality

The FBI will tell you that violent crime has dropped to historic lows. The Justice Policy Institute can show you statistics proving that school shootings remain an extreme rarity. Yet at some level, none of that matters; facts are usually at a disadvantage to perception. And where school violence is concerned, the perception is that things are worse than they have ever been. (Pitts, 2000)

Despite clear statistical evidence that school shootings are rare, many people are convinced that schools are becoming more dangerous and that a shooting of the magnitude of the Columbine tragedy could happen at their local school. A survey conducted by Gallup Poll (Academic Universe Online, 2001) indicated that 65% of adults interviewed believed that a school shooting was somewhat likely or very likely to happen in their community. Another Gallup Poll cited in *USA Today* (Kenworthy & O'Driscoll, 2000) found that 70% of parents with school-age children are more worried about violence since the

Columbine tragedy and about two in five parents are now more involved in monitoring their children's activities.

Because of this perception, fears run high. According to research cited by the American Medical Association, between 1989 and 1996 the percentage of students who feared they would be attacked at school rose from 6% to 9%. Similarly, the percentage of students who avoided one or more places at school out of fear for their own safety climbed from 5% to 9% during that time. A third of high school students stated that they know of a classmate who may be upset enough to perpetrate a violent attack on their school (Lester, 2001). This fear interferes with learning. In a study cited in Arnette and Walsleben (1998), 63% of students reported that they believed they would learn more at school if they felt safer.

The media magnifies the fear felt by parents and students alike. Studies of newspapers and television indicate that the media's coverage of violent crime is out of proportion with its actual occurrence (Dorfman, 2001). Furthermore, the more unusual the crime, the greater the likelihood it will make the evening news. While crime rates are actually dropping, news coverage of violence is increasing. Between 1990 and 1998, homicides dropped by 33% while network television coverage of homicide news increased by an astounding 473% (Dorfman, 2001).

Whether they hold that youth violence is increasing or decreasing, few would argue that violence in our schools is not unacceptably high or that it is not cause for concern. "There is considerable evidence that youth involvement in serious forms of violent behavior is quite stable over time and remains a serious national problem" (U.S. Surgeon General, 2001a).

A Strain of Youth Violence: Schoolplace Violence

The U.S. Secret Service National Threat Assessment Center (2000) refers to the multivictim school homicides as instances of *targeted violence.* Targeted violence is a term developed by the Secret Service to refer to any incident of violence where a known attacker selects a particular target before making a violent attack. The U.S. Secret Service first used this term when looking at individuals who attempted or threatened to assassinate the president. They then stretched this concept to apply to school shooters. In the instances of school shootings, the "target" may be a classmate, teacher, or the school building itself.

Others have called these incidents *rampage* or *spree* killings. In contrast to serial killers, who are methodical and often leave a signature clue in their patterns of homicide, spree killers tend to kill as an act of passion at a frantic pace (Headden & Kulman, 1997). In 2000, the *New York Times* developed a database that analyzed common themes in spree killings. They included many of the multiple–victim school shootings in their sample (Fessenden, 2000). In this database, these school shooters are clustered together with other spree killers such as Charles Whitman, the sniper who shot passersby from the tower at the University of Texas.

We believe that none of these descriptions totally hits the mark in describing the characteristics of the multiple–victim school shooter. These school shooters are more focused than typical spree killers, and yet many of them are not as focused as the name "targeted violence" implies. While many of the school shooters did come to school planning to kill specific individuals, several ended up killing anyone who crossed their paths. As we will explain in more detail later, there are, in these incidents, both victims of choice and victims of opportunity.

Many of the school shooters have characteristics of both targeted–violence and spree killers. Rather than focus on their type of targets, we focus on the psychological dynamics that seem to lead them to act. Our definition of schoolplace violence is "an incident of violence that takes place on school grounds or during a school-related function where a student retaliates against a perceived injustice, becomes an avenger, and uses deadly force against classmates, school staff, or law enforcement." This definition excludes school shootings related to robbery, gang violence, drug–related violence, single–victim suicides, and non–student perpetrators.

Despite popular perception to the contrary, schoolplace violence incidents are rare. The Center for the Study and Prevention of Violence (1999c) states that since 1992 there have been approximately 190 shooting deaths in American schools. These deaths represent only about 1% of all youth killed with guns. Nevertheless, the impact of these events has been tremendous and has changed the culture of our schools and our country.

Many have wondered if schoolplace violence is a passing fad exaggerated by the media, or if it is truly a trend in our society. *Fads* in American culture are very commonplace. They gain much attention in a short period of time and fade out just as quickly. With violence, fads are often created through urban myths. For example, during the mid–1990s, many people lived with the fear of being shot because they flashed their car's headlights at an oncoming car that was driving with no headlights on in the dark. For a few weeks, this myth circulated via the Internet and grapevines. People feared that it was part of some rite of passage for gang members. When this pattern of violence did not materialize, the fad dissolved.

In contrast to fads, *trends* are patterns of violence that alter the norms of our society. When threats and acts of violence are consistent over time, we adapt our way of living to minimize their impact. Our behavior changes. Soon, adjustment becomes second nature, and people do not consider the changes in behavior to be abnormal. One example of a trend in violence involves product tampering. Not too long ago, over-the-counter medication and food products were sold in relatively easy-to-open packaging—at best, childproof caps existed. But after the Tylenol tampering incidents of the 1980s and the numerous copycat crimes that followed, products began to appear on the shelves amply protected with seals and plastic wrapping. This trend has resulted in inconvenience and increased product costs, but the public does not seem to mind. In fact, most of us would not buy a bottle of cough syrup if there was not a protective seal wrapped around it. People have adapted to the security measures necessary, and barely realize a violent trend has changed the norm of our culture.

Airport security is another example of the effects of a trend in violence. Before the 1970s, safety checks were minimal. However, as terrorism, hijacking, and bomb threats increased in frequency throughout the early 1970s, the airline industry was forced to take major steps. Until quite recently, we may have thought of those post–1970s security measures in airports as quite intrusive and intense. Now, of course, after the destruction of September 11, 2001, we have quickly accepted yet another ratcheting up of security measures, and consider the airport routines of the recent past terribly inadequate. We have adapted once again.

It is our contention that regardless of the number of instances that have occurred, schoolplace violence is a trend in our culture. The few school shootings that have taken place may not constitute a verifiable statistical pattern, but they have rattled our collective psyche to such an extent that we are changed forever. The following graph (Figure 1.1) summarizes the trend in schoolplace violence.

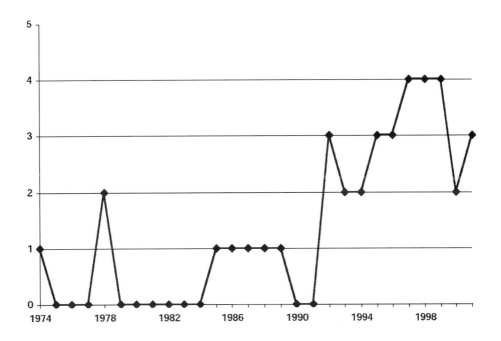

Figure 1.1: Total Number of Violent School Incidents

Schoolplace Violence Chronology

Incidents of schoolplace violence are not a new phenomenon. The earliest incident occurred in 1974 when a student brought a gun and homemade bombs to his school, set off the fire alarm, and shot at janitors and firemen who responded to the alarm. In evaluating the years between 1974 and 2000, the U.S. Secret Service National Threat Assessment Center has identified 37 incidents involving 41 attackers that meet the targeted violence criteria. The targeted violence occurred in 26 states, with more than one incident happening in Arkansas, California, Kentucky, Missouri, and Tennessee. The most infamous cases are summarized here.

January 18, 1993: Grayson, Kentucky

Gary "Scott" Pennington, age 17, entered his seventh-period English class at East Carter High School, fatally shot his teacher, and held the class of 22 students hostage. When a janitor attempted to intervene, he shot the janitor as well. He used his father's .38-caliber pistol. His motive was revenge against the teacher for questioning his increasingly morbid writings. Scott was an honor student and had written in a journal, "They don't give out awards for what I have planned."

January 23, 1995: Redlands, California

After being reprimanded by his principal for violating the school's dress code, John Sirola, age 13, walked home and stole a sawed-off shotgun from a family friend. He immediately returned to Sacred Heart High School, shot the principal, and then killed himself. There is some question as to whether or not his suicide was accidental as witnesses claimed he tripped while fleeing the scene. The principal survived.

October 12, 1995: Blackville, South Carolina

Toby Sincino, age 16, was suspended for making an obscene hand gesture. The next day, he entered the teachers' workroom with a .32-caliber revolver, fatally shot a math teacher, and then committed suicide. Another math teacher died of a heart attack in reaction to the shooting.

November 15, 1995: Lynnville, Tennessee

At Richland High School, Jamie Rouse, age 17, fatally shot a teacher with a .22 rifle. He then shot and killed a student and wounded another teacher. Investigators suggest that the student got in the way of a bullet meant for another teacher. The hunting rifle Rouse used was given to him by his father as a birthday present. The previous day he had been in a car accident and was angry about it. He was also facing mounting academic difficulty. He told an acquaintance about his plans before the shooting.

February 2, 1996: Moses Lake, Washington

Dressed in black and toting a .30-.30 deer rifle, 14-year-old honors student Barry Loukaitis of Frontier Junior High School shot and killed two students and a teacher in an algebra class. He was armed with a rifle, two handguns, and 70 rounds of ammunition. His classmates called Loukaitis, a straight-A student, a "nerd." Reports indicate that he was "relentlessly" teased by one of the students he killed. He was known to pore over gun magazines at the town library. A good deal of evidence has been offered that Loukaitis was influenced by movies (*Natural Born Killers*), books (Stephen King/Richard Bachman's novel *Rage*), and music videos (Pearl Jam's "Jeremy").

February 19, 1997: Bethel, Alaska

After making multiple threats, Evan Ramsey, a 16-year-old student at Bethel Regional High School, chased fellow students through the halls of the school before opening fire with his shotgun. One student and the principal were killed, and two other students were wounded. The student who was killed reportedly had called Ramsey names. After a short standoff with the police, he surrendered.

Unlike many schoolplace violence perpetrators, Ramsey led a life full of chaos and abuse. When he was in high school his grades were poor and friends noted signs of depression. On the day of the killing, he was angry with the principal for taking away his walkie-talkie. He was tired of people calling him names. Before the incident, he told two friends of his intention to bring a gun to school. One of the friends helped him learn how to load and fire a 12-gauge shotgun. Before Ramsey arrived on school premises, a group of students gathered in the second floor library that overlooked the lobby because they were told that something spectacular was going to take place.

October 1, 1997: Pearl, Mississippi

Luke Woodham, age 16, stabbed his mother to death then proceeded to Pearl High School, where he shot nine students. Two of the students, one of them his ex-girlfriend, died. Seven students were wounded. Woodham called himself a "satanic assassin," and witnesses described him as "cool and calm" during the gunfire. Six other students, allegedly involved in a satanic cult with Woodham, were charged with conspiracy to commit murder. He stated that he felt unloved by his mother (his father had left the family years before) and rejected by most kids at school. A triggering event appeared to be his mother's refusal to drive him to a friend's house on the morning of the killing. Before the shooting, he tortured and killed his dog.

The attack was the result of long–term planning. Woodham was prepared to die in his plan, either in a gun battle or by suicide. When an armed assistant principal confronted him during the actual attack, he meekly surrendered, saying, "I don't want to die today."

December 1, 1997: West Paducah, Kentucky

Michael Carneal, age 14, opened fire on a prayer group at Heath High School. He shot and killed three students and wounded others with a .22–caliber semiautomatic pistol. Carneal was well armed with two rifles and two shotguns stolen from his neighbor's garage. Raised in an upper–middle–class family, Carneal was a B student. He had warned friends to stay away from the prayer group, stating, "Something big is going to happen." Before the shooting, he referred to a scene in the movie *The Basketball Diaries* in which someone opens fire on a classroom. As he was wrestled to the ground following the incident, he cried out, "Kill me now!"

December 15, 1997: Stamps, Arkansas

Joseph "Colt" Todd, age 14, sought vengeance on peers who had picked on him. He hid in a wooded area near school grounds, shooting at and wounding two students as they entered Stamps High School. Todd told police that he was not specifically targeting the students he shot.

March 24, 1998: Jonesboro, Arkansas

Mitchell Johnson, age 13, and Andrew "Drew" Golden, age 11, fatally shot four students and a teacher and wounded 10 others. All the victims were female. Johnson and Golden set off a fire alarm to draw their schoolmates outside and concealed themselves in a wooded area adjacent to Westside Middle School. As the students and teachers exited the building, the boys shot at them. Police apprehended the boys running through the woods near the school and found that they were armed with 10 weapons and more than 100 rounds of ammunition. The boys had 4 handguns and 3 rifles from Golden's grandfather, and 3 more guns from his father. They had packed sleeping bags and a radio in their stolen getaway van. In addition, they had packed two bags of potato chips and a stuffed animal.

Both were average students. Before the killing, Johnson had expressed suicidal thoughts and had told others that he had "a lot of killing to do." He also pulled a knife on a student and mentioned to a friend, "Tomorrow you find out if you live or die."

April 24, 1998: Edinboro, Pennsylvania

During a Parker Middle School eighth-grade graduation dance held at a local banquet hall, Andrew Wurst, age 14, shot and killed one teacher, and wounded another teacher and two students. He used his father's .25-caliber handgun. Before the event, he told others about his desire to kill people and kill himself. He had shown a friend a gun he kept in a dresser.

May 21, 1998: Springfield, Oregon

A student of Thurston High School, Kipland "Kip" Kinkel, age 15, murdered both of his parents in their home and then proceeded to watch the comedy cartoon *South Park.* Shortly after, he drove to school and opened fire on his classmates in the cafeteria. Two students were fatally shot and 23 others wounded. Kinkel used a .22-caliber semi-automatic rifle and two handguns, and he wore a trench coat during the rampage. Witnesses stated that "His face was casual, like it was something he did every day."

Kinkel's motivation was revenge. He was angry with his peers for teasing him, with his parents for confiscating his guns, and with the school for expelling him. About a week before the murders, Kinkel's parents had grounded him for the summer for defacing neighborhood houses with toilet paper. The police had once questioned him for throwing rocks at cars from a freeway overpass. After the killings, the police found five bombs, a hand grenade, and a howitzer shell casing in Kinkel's home. The bombs were homemade and described as "very sophisticated."

April 20, 1999: Littleton, Colorado

Eric Harris, age 18, and Dylan Klebold, age 17, stormed Columbine High School heavily armed with a semiautomatic rifle, two sawed-off shotguns, a semiautomatic handgun, and dozens of homemade bombs. They fired randomly at students and teachers, and then hunted down and killed students who were hiding in various places. Before they killed themselves, they murdered 12 students and a teacher, and wounded 23 others. The boys were known to play violent video games, visit grotesque and sexually deviant Web sites, and listen to music filled with themes of hate and destruction. They were angry with peers who called them names such as "dirtbags, faggots, and inbreeds." They hung out with a loosely associated group of nonconformists called the "Trench Coat Mafia."

Both boys had been convicted of felonies before the attack. Allegedly, at some point in the year before the massacre, Harris's father found a pipe bomb in his son's room, but did not call the police. After the killings, a diary was found detailing their desire to kill 500 people at Columbine, and then, in a twist that now looks bizarrely prophetic, to hijack a plane to crash into New York City. The diary contained one year's worth of planning for the attack, and there were maps of the school showing places to hide and the location of the largest concentration of students at a particular time.

This case caused international concern about school violence in America and became a turning point. After the tragedy at Columbine the fear of "it could happen here" became a real concern for students, parents, administrators, and communities all over the country. Evidence of the extent to which this tragedy has affected our culture can be heard in changes in our language. Just as the term "going postal" evolved out of the post-office shootings, the term "pulling a Columbine" is gaining popularity. *Time* magazine headlined this phenomenon "The Columbine Effect" on the cover of the March 2001 issue.

May 20, 1999: Conyers, Georgia

Thomas Solomon Jr., age 15, had been heard telling his classmates that he would "blow up this classroom" and that he had no reason to live. Solomon was being treated for depression and reported being teased by a popular sports player at the school. Solomon believed that this individual was the object of his girlfriend's affections. On May 20, Solomon went to school at Heritage High School with his stepfather's .22 rifle and wounded six students.

November 19, 1999: Deming, New Mexico

The day before coming to Deming Middle School armed with a firearm, Victor Cordova Jr., age 12, was heard boasting that he would "make history blasting this school." No one reported Cordova's threats, and the next day he brought a gun to school and fired one shot into the school's lobby, hitting a student who died the next day.

December 6, 1999: Fort Gibson, Oklahoma

Seth Trickey, age 13, was obsessed by the military and reported being deeply influenced by the Columbine shootings. Trickey came to school armed with his father's 9-mm semiautomatic handgun and fired approximately 15 rounds into a group of students. Four students were wounded.

May 26, 2000: Lake Worth, Florida

After being sent home for throwing water balloons, Nathaniel Brazill, age 13, returned to school with a .25 semiautomatic handgun. He then went into an English class and shot and killed the teacher. Prior to the shooting, Brazill had shown other students the gun and talked about having hit lists.

March 5, 2001: Santee, California

Charles Andrew Williams, age 15, was a bullied teenager with a history of drug use. Reportedly Williams told at least a dozen people, including one adult, that there would be a shoot-out at the school. People believed Williams when he told them he was just joking. When Williams came to school on March 5, he began shooting at students from a bathroom at Santana High School. Williams killed two students and wounded 13 others.

By many accounts, Santana was well prepared to prevent a school shooting. They had well-trained safety officers, conflict resolution courses, threat reporting procedures, and ample counseling services. Nevertheless, the people who knew about the danger did not step forward to report it to authorities.

March 7, 2001: Williamsport, Pennsylvania

Elizabeth Catherine Bush, age 14, became the first female to fit the criteria as a perpetrator of schoolplace violence. She had been threatened and teased mercilessly at her old school in Jersey Shore and had transferred in the spring to Bishop Neumann Catholic School. At Bishop Neumann, Bush was reportedly still being teased. She took her father's revolver into the cafeteria and shot a female classmate in the shoulder. As Bush fired the gun, she is alleged to have said, "No one thought I would go through with this."

Schoolplace Violence, Workplace Violence

What Are the Similarities and Differences?

It is necessary to look at some instances of workplace violence in order to compare the similarities and differences between workplace violence and schoolplace violence. Consider the following examples:

August 20, 1986: Edmond, Oklahoma

Patrick Sherrill, the man credited with starting the concept known as "going postal," entered the Edmond post office carrying two .45-caliber pistols, a .22-caliber handgun, and over 300 rounds of ammunition. His first victim was his shift supervisor who he calmly shot. He then proceeded to kill 14 other employees. Sherrill ended his rampage by committing suicide. He was a member of the marksmanship team with the National Guard Armory and frequently wore combat fatigues. He had a history of habitual complaining, animal maltreatment, and a reputation as a loner and a strange individual. He had no history of a formal diagnosis of mental illness.

February 16, 1988: Sunnyvale, California

Obsessed with coworker Laura Black, Richard Wade Farley became more aggressive and harassing with each rejection of his advances. Repeatedly over the course of a couple of years, he publicly threatened her life and those of other employees. A repeated veiled threat warned his potential targets about his gun collection. On one occasion he sent a letter to Laura in which he warned: "Once I'm fired, you won't be able to control me ever again. Pretty soon, I'll crack under the pressure and run amok and destroy everything in my path." On the day of the shooting, Farley armed himself with a rifle, two handguns, ammunition strapped to his chest, and gasoline. He killed seven employees and wounded four more, including Laura, who managed to escape by running into an adjoining office. Farley had no close friends and no prior criminal record.

June 5, 1997: Santa Fe Springs, California

Daniel Marsden got into an argument with another employee at the plastics company where he worked. He then proceeded to walk through the building randomly shooting, killing two employees and wounding four others. He could be heard mumbling, "I am not a fag," repeatedly. After he finished shooting, Marsden drove to South Los Angeles, brandished his gun at several people, announced, "This is my last day," then shot himself. Others described him as a reclusive loner who was quiet, temperamental, and weird. In an unrelated incident eight days later, another workplace violence incident occurred nearby. A laid-off worker killed a woman, wounded his prior boss, and then committed suicide about 5 miles away from the Marsden shooting.

April 7, 1999: Ottawa, Ontario, Canada

Pierre Lebrun, an ex-bus driver, showed up at his former workplace with a rifle and opened fire on his former coworkers. He killed four and injured two before turning the gun on himself. Lebrun carried a list of potential victims to target, and left a suicide note at home. Police called his rampage "planned and deliberate."

What Are the Similarities?

Most episodes of schoolplace violence have followed the dynamics of adult workplace violence in that the perpetrators had similar motives and gave off warning signs of impending upheaval. Almost all perpetrators of school and workplace shootings made threats or threatening statements prior to committing violence. When compared to patterns of behavior in other types of violence, this behavior looks unusual. Robbers do not warn bank tellers before they strike. Rapists may test their victims before attacking, but they do not often make statements such as "I'm going to rape so-and-so" to their peers.

Most incidents involved white male perpetrators who experienced interpersonal difficulties, had histories of being disgruntled, possessed few coping mechanisms, and were fascinated by and/or proficient with weapons and violence (see Table 1.1). In the two types of violence, the pathways to violence are similar. In both workplace and schoolplace violence, a shooting spree becomes the only conceivable solution to the perpetrators' problems. This avenger mentality, described by McGee and DeBernardo (n.d.), also sets them apart from other perpetrators. In other forms of violence the perpetrator often comes from a position of being socially dominant (as in domestic violence and child abuse) and exerts power over the victims. In workplace and schoolplace violence, the perpetrator is often someone who sees himself or herself as being low in the social hierarchy.

Table 1.1: Shared Characteristics in Perpetrators of Workplace and Schoolplace Violence	
Workplace	**Schoolplace**
Mostly Caucasian men	Mostly Caucasian adolescent boys
History of perceived injustices; filed grievances	Precipitating event: social rejection, school expulsion, disciplinary action
Unsuccessful personal history	Subjected to bullying
Fascination with military, weaponry	Interest in violent music/movies/videos; interest in or experience with weapons

The physical structures of schools and workplaces have additional similarities. Most schools and many workplaces offer ample areas for concealment of the perpetrators. They often have multiple entrance and exit points from which to instigate an attack or to retreat.

In both scenarios, the events tend to unfold very quickly. In both workplace and schoolplace violence the shooting is usually over in a matter of minutes; negotiators and law enforcement have little time to organize a tactical response. Once the perpetrators decide to become violent, there is usually little opportunity for negotiation. The assailants are not concerned about getting caught.

Other factors shared by workplace and schoolplace violence are the organizational issues that may have contributed to the deadly outcome. For example, historically many schools and workplaces have had weak or nonexistent policies against all forms of violence. Over the past decade, with the increase in concern about violence, many institutions have developed such policies, but even in those cases the policies may not be widely known, or may still have kinks to be worked out. Despite awareness of the potential for danger, most people caught in events of this kind continue to express shock in words that have become familiar to us all: "I never thought it could happen here."

Violence prevention training for employees, in the case of workplace violence, and for students, in the case of schoolplace violence, tends to be sporadic or based on long–term prevention (e.g., changing values) rather than on strategies to deal with violence in the here–and–now (e.g., "What do I do when someone threatens to blow up the school?"). Many school and work settings do not have an effective mechanism for report-ing threats or violent behavior. When threats do occur, authorities may fail to take immediate corrective action. If they do take corrective action, they may not adequately secure the building in the aftermath.

What Are the Differences?

While the similarities between workplace and schoolplace violence are striking, there are important differences that change the nature of prevention, interruption, and response procedures in the two environ-ments. Businesses, for example, have a better ability to enact lockdown and secure their facilities. Unless they have trained for it, schools have a more difficult task than in the workplace when trying to achieve lockdown. After all, schools are and continue to be open to the public, and in trying to achieve an open and welcoming environment, schools may keep their facilities accessible late at night and on weekends. Most workplaces are not open to the public, and most are well secured. In this respect, workplaces may have an edge over schools in their ability to avert tragedy.

But several of the differences between schools and professional workplaces point to the greater opportunities for prevention efforts in schools. For example, students have less access to weapons than do adult workers. The school population consists mostly of minors, who are not allowed to purchase firearms. When students bring guns to school, someone else is usually involved. It is likely that a parent or family member has not secured the family firearm, or that, as in the case of Columbine High School, someone of age has purchased the gun for the minor. These obstacles are not present for the adult workplace violence perpetrator.

For the most part, students have someone else responsible for their whereabouts and behavior. Parents can play a significant role in helping their schools become safer environments. Parental communication and participation are important factors in a collaborative effort to maintain safe schools. In workplace violence, family members tend to be involved only when they are victims of domestic violence.

The relationship between students and school staff differs significantly from that between an employee and employers. By their nature, schools are actively involved with students on a daily basis. Because schools are learning environments, school personnel may be inclined to give students a second chance after a serious threat has been made, with the hope that the student can learn from his or her mistakes. This may be violence prevention of the most basic and hopeful kind.

How Is Schoolplace Violence Affecting the Culture of Our Schools?

Like airline terrorism and product tampering, schoolplace violence appears to be another rare form of violence that has become a trend in our society. The violent events themselves we call "low frequency, high impact." In these trends the instances are isolated at first. Then the events begin to increase in frequency and intensity.

Increased media attention has expanded the impact of these events. Millions of people are now affected as the images of terrified escaping students, distraught school communities, and riveting trials are replayed over and over in our living rooms. These events and their media coverage have substantially changed how we view schools and youth.

Furthermore, this form of violence is changing day–to–day school operations. Schools are implementing the use of metal detectors, increased school security, and school dress codes. Most schools are developing emergency plans to deal with this type of crisis. Here are some of the violence prevention precautions implemented by schools directly affected by schoolplace violence:

- **Redlands, California:** After the shooting death of a principal at Sacred Heart School, the Redlands community developed several programs to prevent teen violence. Their "Building a Generation" program surveyed teenagers to find out what was lacking in their lives, then attempted to provide what they needed. A peer counseling and mediation program addresses issues of conflict resolution. A software company called Environmental Systems Research Institute now provides the means to learn which parts of town are seeing an escalation in teen–related problems.

- **Edinboro, Pennsylvania:** In the aftermath of the murder of a middle school teacher, this school implemented a community coalition to fund anger–management classes. The school also revised its curriculum and student conduct handbook in ways that may help prevent future violence problems. To increase security efforts, the school staff currently wear identification badges, and all school doors except the main entrance are locked during the day.

- **Jonesboro, Arkansas:** Some districts have hired local police to patrol their campuses, while other schools have hired new social workers to provide conflict resolution training for teachers. Lawmakers in Arkansas are debating legislation that would make guns less accessible to minors.

- **Springfield, Oregon:** Pending concerns about confidentiality, the Springfield school district is considering providing school personnel with information about students with histories of violent behavior and criminal records.

- **Moses Lake, Washington:** Frontier Junior High School took additional security measures and renovated the school building. They widened hallways to eliminate concealment and loitering opportunities. Surveillance cameras monitor all areas in the school. School personnel now wear badges and security guards patrol the halls.

Chapter Two

The Dynamics of Schoolplace Violence

We will be using the following terms to discuss the participants involved in schoolplace violence:

Perpetrator: A violent individual, or one who poses an immediate threat.

Targets: The potential recipients of violent actions.

Victims: Actual recipients of the violence.

Protectors: Individuals within the school community who can identify, prevent, or defuse a potentially violent situation.

Perpetrators

Perpetrators of schoolplace violence appear to consist largely of adolescent white male students from 11 to 21 years of age. They initially may display a "victim mentality," though at some point they take on the "avenger mentality." Table 2.1 (page 30) summarizes the characteristics of perpetrators.

Most of the perpetrators gave significant warning signs of their pending attack. Many of them told others the details of what they intended to do; others made threats. These warning signs were *boundary probing.* When they were not taken seriously, the perpetrators pushed the boundary of their violent behavior from words to action.

Table 2.1: Characteristics of Schoolplace Violence Perpetrators	
Demographics	**Percentage**
Sex: Male	97%
Race: Caucasian	75%
Age: Preadolescent to Adolescent (11–21)	100%
Characteristics	
• Planned the attack.	>66%
• Made verbal threats prior to the incident.	>75%
• Told someone prior to the attack.	100%
• Told more than one person.	50%
• Brought a gun from home.	66%
• Had diffulty coping.	>75%
• Held a grievance.	>75%
• Was teased/felt victimized.	>66%
• Was suicidal.	50%
• Had a history of feeling depressed.	>50%
• Was influenced/encouraged by others.	>50%
• Had a history of drug/alcohol abuse.	<33%

Source: Adapted from U.S. Secret Service National Threat Assessment Center (2000).

Many of these perpetrators, like the workplace violence perpetrators, held grievances and felt unjustly treated by others. The gun became their great equalizer.

Unlike other types of violent crime, substance abuse does not play a major role for most perpetrators. Many, however, were depressed or suicidal, and it has been suggested that this act may be a form of *suicide-by-cop* (see chapter 5). This term is used to describe what happens when an individual attempts to provoke a police officer to use deadly force.

Killing Teams

There may be a new fad or trend in schoolplace violence: killing teams. While other schoolplace violence perpetrators had accomplices in the wings, only the Jonesboro and Columbine tragedies had two individuals involved in the actual shooting. Killing teams are a serious departure from other episodes and represent a more lethal picture.

The psychological dynamics of team killers are inherently different from those associated with single perpetrators. Two individuals devising such a plan together are likely to experience a social reinforcement aspect and added pressure to not let each other down. They also reinforce each other's perceptions of perceived injustices, propagating a sense of "us" versus "them." These dynamics increase the chances that the perpetrators will execute their plan. In addition, when there are more perpetrators, there likely will be a higher number of victims. With more guns and more bombs, more people can be targeted.

When it comes to intervention, there are two directions killing teams can take. On one hand, with two perpetrators involved in the actual violent spree, many opportunities to intervene are circumvented. For instance, one perpetrator can keep watch for law enforcement while the other continues. Ambush tactics are also easier to carry out with two perpetrators. On the other hand, probability of detection is increased because there are more chances for a *leak* of information. The more people involved, the greater the likelihood that someone will start talking about the plans, and they will be thwarted.

Victims

Who were the victims of these violent rampages? They were teachers, principals, janitors, ex-girlfriends, hated peers, and innocent bystanders. The large majority of the victims, roughly 82%, have been students. Approximately 14% were teachers, principals, and other staff members, and about 1% were parents. From 1974 to 1996, 64% of the victims in schoolplace violence were students and 36% were staff members. From 1997 to 2001 these figures shifted: 87% of the victims were students and 7% were staff members. Table 2.2 (pages 32–33) summarizes the characteristics of the victims of schoolplace violence since 1974.

Victims of Choice

A *victim of choice* is the direct target of the assailant, the one against whom the perpetrator is seeking revenge. In most of the schoolplace violence tragedies of the past few years, victims of choice were often

Table 2.2: Characteristics of Schoolplace Violence Victims

Place of School Violence	Total Dead	Total Injured	Student Victims	School Staff Victims	Parent Victims	Attackers Committed Suicide?
Olean, NY	1	0	0	0	0	Yes
Austin, TX	1	0	0	1	0	No
Lanett, AL	0	1	0	1	0	No
Goddard, KS	4	0	3	1	0	No
Lewiston, MT	1	3	2	2	0	No
Dekalb, MO	2	0	1	0	0	Yes
Virginia Beach, VA	1	1	0	2	0	No
Orange County, CA	0	1	1	0	0	No
Olivehurst, CA	4	13	16	1	0	No
Napa, CA	0	2	2	0	0	No
Great Barrington, MA	2	4	6	0	0	No
Grayson, KY	2	0	0	2	0	No
Wauwatosa, WI	1	0	0	1	0	No
Greensboro, NC	0	1	0	1	0	Yes
Manchester, IA	0	1	0	1	0	No
Redlands, CA	1	1	0	1	0	Yes
Blackville, SC	3	0	0	2	0	Yes
Lynnville, TN	2	1	1	2	0	No
Moses Lake, WA	3	1	3	1	0	No
Palo Alto, CA	1	3	3	0	0	Yes
Patterson, MO	1	0	1	0	0	No

Table 2.2: Characteristics of Schoolplace Violence Victims (continued)

Place of School Violence	Total Dead	Total Injured	Student Victims	School Staff Victims	Parent Victims	Attackers Committed Suicide?
Scottsdale, AZ	1	0	0	1	0	No
Bethel, AK	2	2	3	1	0	No
Pearl, MS	3	7	9	0	1 (mo)	No
West Paducah, KY	3	5	8	0	0	No
Stamps, AR	0	2	2	0	0	No
Jonesboro, AR	5	10	12	2	0	No
Edinboro, PA	1	3	2	2	0	No
Fayetteville, TN	1	0	1	0	0	No
Springfield, OR	4	23	25	0	2 (mo & fa)	No
Littleton, CO	15	23	35	3	0	Yes (2)
Conyers, GA	0	6	6	0	0	No
Deming, NM	1	0	1	0	0	No
Fort Gibson, OK	0	4	4	0	0	No
Lake Worth, FL	1	0	0	1	0	No
Oxnard, CA	1	0	0	0	0	No
Santee, CA	2	13	15	0	0	No
Williamsport, PA	0	1	1	0	0	No
TOTALS	70	132	163	29	3	7

| Table 2.3: Victim of Choice Profiles ||
Perpetrators	Victims of Choice
Gary "Scott" Pennington	English teacher
John Sirola	Principal
Toby Sincino	Principal
Evan Ramsey	Principal, a student who picked on him
Luke Woodham	Mother, ex-girlfriend, students who picked on him
Joseph "Colt" Todd	Peers who picked on him
Mitchell Johnson	Ex-girlfriend
Kip Kinkel	Parents, peers who teased him

identified either specifically (e.g., the principal) or generally (e.g., peers who picked on the perpetrator) (see Table 2.3). Consistently in school-place violence the victims of choice have been chosen as targets of revenge, often following a history or instance of rejection. Ironically, Eric Harris, one of the Columbine perpetrators, amassed a hit list of approximately 15 students who had enraged him before the shooting, but not one of these targeted victims of choice was wounded or killed in the attack.

Victims of Opportunity

A *victim of opportunity* is an individual who is not targeted, but who happens to be in the vicinity when the violence occurs. In many instances, victims of opportunity far outnumber victims of choice. This could be because the victim of choice is not readily available, or because the victim of opportunity gets in the way of the target. For example, in the case in Grayson, Kentucky, Scott Pennington shot and killed a janitor who tried to intervene. In many cases, even when the victim of choice is available and has been attacked, the perpetrator gains momentum through the act of violence and redirects the attack toward the next available person. This pattern was clearly evident with Eric Harris and Dylan Klebold who cheered one another on as they continued their spree.

Some victims of opportunity are caught in the crossfire or suffer unintended harm from the perpetrator. In the Blackville, South Carolina, case, Toby Sincino intended to kill the principal who had suspended him. Instead, he shot and killed a teacher, and another teacher subsequently died of a heart attack from the stress of the event.

There seems to be a pattern developing in the balance of victims of choice and victims of opportunity. When schoolplace violence incidents first surfaced, the targets of choice were more often principals and teachers, while the victims of opportunity (e.g., students and other staff) had usually tried to obstruct the perpetrator. Since then, the perpetrators' scope of victims of choice has expanded to include more generalized peer groups. Because there are more victims of choice, the potential exists for exponentially more victims of opportunity. For example, if a perpetrator sought revenge on one classmate, that classmate would be the victim of choice. The potential victims of opportunity would be all the other students in the same vicinity at the time of the shooting. Because of their proximity, these victims of opportunity are at risk for stray and deflected bullets, shrapnel from bombs, and hostage situations. Now consider the situation if the perpetrator has 4 or even 40 victims of choice. The potential number of victims is staggering.

Degrees of Victimization

The ripple effect of trauma impacts a wide circle of potential victims. (We treat this effect in more detail in chapter 13.) *Primary victims* are those individuals who have experienced the violence directly. These are the people who are actually attacked or threatened during the assault. *Secondary victims* are the friends, witnesses, parents, rescue personnel, and others who are involved but not directly impacted by the violence. These secondary victims are often overlooked in trauma recovery efforts, but many of them may experience a posttraumatic response.

Tertiary victims are the helpers who also become affected by the violent event. In the aftermath of a violent incident, counselors may be flooded with individuals in crisis, needs for debriefing sessions, and requests for consultation. At the same time these professionals may be dealing with their own reactions to the trauma. They may also be vicariously affected by listening to story after story from the survivors. In some cases counselors may internalize another's pain and become overwhelmed, exhibiting posttraumatic symptoms like those of their clients.

The *fourth-degree victims* are found at the community level. Many victims of school shootings and their families are deeply integrated into the surrounding community. The victims and their families are church members, employees, neighbors, volunteers, and patrons of local businesses. These community establishments also experience shock and grief, and the community as a whole suffers and mourns.

Protectors

Protectors are those individuals or agencies that stand between potential perpetrators and their ability to commit violence. Protectors build insulation around possible victims not just when the shooting is occurring, but in the early stages when potential perpetrators are making threats. There are formal protectors who are trained in their profession to de-escalate and interrupt violent situations. There are also informal protectors who rise to the occasion because they feel that it is the right thing to do, and because they have the skills and courage to do it.

Protectors can include

- Administrators
- Teachers
- Students
- Mentors
- Coaches
- Counselors
- School support staff
- Parents
- Emergency rescue personnel
- Public safety officers

Predicting Violence

Schoolplace violence is to some degree random, but it is also, we now understand, predictable in certain potentially useful ways. It may in fact be possible to deflect some potential perpetrators before they become dangerous to others. After all, a hospitable set of circumstances must exist before any perpetrator can commit an act of schoolplace violence. The formula that has been developed to assess the possibility of violence is identified by the acronym **TOADS**:

> **T**ime
>
> **O**pportunity
>
> **A**bility
>
> **D**esire
>
> **S**timulus

Each of these factors can be measured or controlled by the school administration, or by the professionals who assess the dangerousness of the situation. In expanded form, TOADS adds up to the following:

Time

A perpetrator must have sufficient time in which to complete an act of violence. The individual must have time to formulate and design a plan, overcome any inhibitions about engaging in violence, gain access to the intended victim or victims, and execute the act. In many ways, time was an ally for Eric Harris and Dylan Klebold. They spent a full year planning the attack on their classmates. Rather than risk impediment by the chance factors of an impulsive spree, they planned their assault to coincide with times when large groups of students would be congregating in the cafeteria and library. Because the attack caught so many people off guard, Harris and Klebold had ample time to move freely about the school and execute their detailed plan. Protectors can remove the time factor from the equation by responding quickly to threats and other concerning or inappropriate behaviors. *Protectors can interrupt these practice sessions for violence before the episodes occur.*

Opportunity

Opportunity is the chance, or opening, that allows the perpetrator access to the target. This factor can be disabled by swift intervention by protectors in the school community. In those instances where the perpetrator is known, his or her access to school property must be controlled. Posting a photograph of the suspect at entryways and, in cases of severe threat, hiring outside security or using the community resource police officer usually accomplishes this.

The media gives a lot of attention to instances where school systems failed to protect children, and shooting tragedies occurred. What the public does not hear about are the many successful interventions where school officials have appropriately responded to threats and removed the perpetrator's opportunity. For example, in Racine, Wisconsin, a principal circulated a memo urging students to report any threats or instances of disturbing behavior to school officials. Within a week, a potential school shooting was thwarted when someone overheard some teens discussing plans to shoot up Burlington High School. This group of students was subsequently ordered to seek counseling.

In another instance, a potential perpetrator's opportunity was taken away when someone anonymously advised a middle school principal that a student had concealed a 9-mm handgun in his locker. When the police interviewed the student, they discovered that he was also hiding a fully loaded magazine in his homeroom desk. The student was subsequently arrested, suspended, and hospitalized for a psychiatric evaluation. In chapter 3, we discuss what we know about *near misses* like this one.

Ability

The level of threat increases in direct proportion to the perpetrator's ability to commit a violent act. This involves both the requisite physical expertise and the mental capability to formulate and execute a plan of action. When assessing a potential perpetrator's ability, one must take into account intelligence, creativity, and organizational skills; experience with and access to weaponry; hand-eye coordination; and desensitization to violence.

Intelligence and Creativity

The majority of schoolplace violence perpetrators have possessed average to above-average intelligence. A student's intelligence can be inferred from teacher reports and academic records. The student's level of organization is also important here. A perpetrator may have a great deal of intellectual ability, yet be so disorganized as to be unable to adequately plan and carry out a violent act. In the histories of schoolplace violence offenders, several honor students emerge in the group. In the Columbine High School case, both Eric Harris and Dylan Klebold were above-average students whose combination of intellect, creativity, and violent motives became a reoccurring theme throughout their high school careers. For example, Harris developed his own hate-filled Web site. The two students collaborated on video projects that depicted them attacking a house with toy guns and shooting real guns at trees. They wrote extensively about rocket launchers, grenades, shotguns, bullets, and death in their class papers. Prior to the massacre, they applied their intelligence to creating explosive devices and planning their attack.

Weapons Proficiency

The individual who threatens to shoot someone must have the gun knowledge and skill necessary to carry out that threat. Among the documented perpetrators of schoolplace violence, most had previous experience with weapons. For many with prior experience, the interest usually extended beyond the occasional hunting foray with friends and relatives. An obsession with weapons or violence had developed. Gun proficiency in homes where hunting and target shooting are common practices is not usually cause for concern. However, when someone becomes totally consumed with the study of weapons in their many aspects, the potential for violence increases.

Bomb Proficiency: A Red Flag for Violence

A definite indicator of the potential for violence is proficiency with explosives. Prosocial use of explosives by teenagers, beyond the usual Fourth of July fireworks, is virtually unheard of. In the recent history of schoolplace violence, Kip Kinkel, Eric Harris, and Dylan Klebold had all become experts at assembling pipe bombs and other explosive devices.

Bombs clearly offer a chance for "maximum killing power," as Harris bragged. Of course, part of the media fallout with this incident was the advertisement of the Internet as a source of information and instruction on how to make a bomb. Such media attention increases the risk that copycat schoolplace violence incidents will continue this threat. The presence of bombs complicates law enforcement intervention because, in a sense, the police are out-armed. Although a student's interest in guns should not necessarily give rise to suspicion, an interest in bombs is cause for grave concern. There are no prosocial uses for bombs.

Hand-Eye Coordination and Desensitization to Violence

Military officers preparing for combat are often trained with violence simulators that help prepare them, mentally and physically, for real battle. Police psychologists train police officers through the use of "high fidelity" role-playing. The officers are put in a threatening situation and are instructed to use components of peak performance to assess and respond to the situation. This psychological and physiological rehearsal helps them learn to control their physiological states in order to maximize their mental and physical abilities.

Mental rehearsal is an essential aspect of peak performance, and athletes have long used this technique to improve their performance. They attempt to get all senses involved in this imagery task to make it as vivid and accurate as possible—skiers seeing themselves slaloming perfectly down a hill, equestrians picturing themselves flawlessly clearing every obstacle. Violent perpetrators rehearse also, visualizing the details of their planned attacks repeatedly in their minds.

There may be a parallel between these training modes and the intense "training" that today's youth receive from violent video games. These games offer the same skills as the training methods: hand-eye coordination, desensitization to violence, visualization, self-control, and mental rehearsal. Eric Harris and Dylan Klebold demonstrated how this phenomenon could be transferred from fantasy to reality. Harris had mastered the video game "Doom" and its even more violent sequel "Doom 2." He took this game a step further by creating floor plans designed as new levels of the game. These new combat zones reportedly resembled Harris's neighborhood and Columbine High School. The scenes he created climaxed with mass killing during which the player could switch into "God mode" to become invincible.

Michael Carneal was reported to have extensive experience with simulated guns through playing video games such as "Doom" and "Quake." Before the day of the murders, he had never fired a real pistol in his life. When he fired his gun at the prayer circle in West Paducah, Kentucky, he did so with remarkable accuracy. He fired eight shots and hit eight targets.

While there has been quite a debate about the effects of video game and movie violence, recent evidence suggests that both desensitization and improved hand–eye coordination are attributable to experience with these video games. The National Institute on Media and the Family (1999) comments that while video games have several positive applications for children (e.g., introducing them to technology, opportunities to practice logic, and entertainment), many of the games may confuse reality and fantasy while fostering social isolation. A multitude of studies, including those published by the *School Psychology Review* (Hughes, 1996) and Mediascope (n.d.), a nonprofit organization funded by the Carnegie and California Wellness Foundations, also support the notion that viewing violence is linked to violent behavior.

Even defenders of violent video games are indirectly supporting these claims. One anonymous video game proponent wrote in an essay for his English class, "Games are a good way for kids to develop good hand–eye coordination and good timing. Without killer reflexes and good aim, one will find some difficulty trying to conquer any action game. Killer reflexes and good aim not only serve to make you better at video games but can help in sports and the military."

Retired Army Lieutenant Colonel David Grossman, a national expert on the psychology of killing, believes that the visual violence plaguing our culture is breeding a nation of "natural–born" killers. He was a Pulitzer Prize nominee for his book, *On Killing: The Psychological Cost of Learning to Kill in War and Society*. Grossman, a psychology professor who has taught at West Point and now teaches at Arkansas State University in Jonesboro, was among the first counselors to arrive on the scene after the Jonesboro shootings. Grossman likens visual violence to an addictive substance, and says that the experience offered by violent video games is very similar to that created by drill sergeants striving to turn recruits into killing machines. Specifically, he claims that "point-and-shoot" video games are remarkably similar to military training devices. Grossman says that the Army knows that these techniques condition a soldier to fire reflexively to overcome the natural tendencies not to kill (McGibbon, 1999).

One troubling video game called "Postal" actually seems to give players the script for a workplace or schoolplace violence massacre. In this game, a disgruntled, raincoat-clad man shoots down police, church-goers, pedestrians, and other innocent bystanders while muttering "going postal." The game especially rewards the killing of law enforcement targets by moving the player to a higher level each time such a target is hit. In the end, the "postal dude" must commit suicide to win the game.

According to Grossman, "brutalization" is the first step in developing violent individuals. Learning to exhibit stoicism and even pleasure in the face of human suffering comes next. Eric Harris frequently visited Web sites that showed graphic pictures of real human death and dismemberment. These pictures were accompanied by captions that glorified the gore and horror of the subject matter. Sexual brutality further objectified the bodies in many pictures. Evidence suggests that desensitization caused by exposure to these forms of visual violence can strengthen a person's mental ability to carry out destruction and violence.

Desire

The desire to inflict injury or death on a person or persons must be present at a serious level in perpetrators of schoolplace violence. The desire usually builds within the individual to the point that he or she perceives it as overwhelming and feels a sense of urgency to act out violently. Revenge is an omnipresent and consistent theme in school-place violence. Two-thirds of the shooters felt bullied or persecuted and three-fourths had difficulty coping with major change (U.S. Secret Service National Threat Center, 2000). The psychological fragility of these adolescents makes them particularly vulnerable to rejection and taunting from peers.

Feeling powerless, these vulnerable teens begin to concoct elaborate fantasies of revenge. The fantasies can become highly developed, with details about the victims, witnesses, times, places, and the actual dynamics of the violent act. Such fantasies become for them a primary coping mechanism, and their ability to problem-solve is increasingly narrowed. The satisfaction they derive from these thoughts only goes so far, however, and the soon-to-be-perpetrators move toward acting on their revenge fantasies.

The desire to act on the fantasy becomes a mission. Eric Harris wrote on his Web site, "We plan out and execute missions. Anyone pisses us off, we do a little deed to their house. We have many enemies in our school, therefore, we make many missions. . . . I will rig up explosives all over a town and detonate each one of them at will . . . ."

On the computer, Eric Harris could cultivate his desire to kill. He could expose his rage to a world full of strangers. He had the freedom to do and say as he pleased without consequences. As *Westword* reporter Alan Prendergast (1999) has noted, Harris reinvented himself to become even more powerful and intimidating than the bullies he despised. The changes in Harris's Web site moniker track this evolution. In his first America Online profile, he called himself "Rebldomakr" or "Rebel Doom Maker." In his later profile, he called himself "Reb Domine" or "Lord of the Rebels."

Harris and Klebold were also known to favor a German band's violent lyrics so much that they become known by others as the Rammstein Boyz. Among the lyrics of the German group we find the following: "You in the schoolyard/I'm ready to kill and nobody here knows of my loneliness. . . . We announce Doomsday/There will be no mercy/Run, run for your lives. . . . You believe killing might be hard/But where are all the dead coming from?" (Prendergast, 1999).

Desire feeds fantasy, which then feeds desire. The perpetrator seems unable to tell fantasy from reality, and the results have been deadly.

Table 2.4: Possible Triggering Events	
John Sirola	Principal reprimand
Toby Sincino	Suspended for obscene hand gesture the day before
Jamie Rouse	Traffic accident the day before
Evan Ramsey	Disciplinary action by the principal
Luke Woodham	Girlfriend broke up with him
Mitchell Johnson	Breakup with girlfriend
Kip Kinkel	Expelled from school the day before for gun possession

Stimulus

The stimulus is the event, or series of events, that will become an internal or external trigger for the violence. The stimulus can often be anticipated, which allows a preparation plan to be implemented. A common trigger for adolescents is the breakup of a romantic relationship. Faced with overwhelming feelings of rejection and abandonment and possessing only minimal coping skills, the student is unable to handle his emotions. Another frequently seen trigger is the encountering of some kind of trouble in school or within the legal system—trouble that will have unwanted consequences for the individual. The individual may feel there is no viable alternative to violence. See Table 2.4 for some of the schoolplace violence perpetrators' triggers.

The phenomenon of *copycat* violence applies here as well. That is, the act of a single perpetrator may inspire similar acts by others. That adolescents are particularly susceptible to this phenomenon seems clearly evidenced by the statistically documented increase in youth suicides following the suicide of one young person. A similar trend is observed in episodes of schoolplace violence.

Critical Period

The *critical period* is the amount of time a potential target is especially vulnerable to an act of violence. The critical period generally ranges from 24 hours to 2 or 3 weeks following the triggering event that is the point after which the perpetrator decides that violence is a reasonable alternative.

Although it has not occurred in schoolplace violence yet, an issue that has affected workplace violence is the *anticipation* of a triggering event. Such anticipation can extend the critical period to include a period of days *before* the stimulus. For example, in February 2001, a 66-year-old ex-employee of Navistar in Elk Grove, Illinois, shot and killed four workers and wounded four others before killing himself. His trigger? A 5-month prison sentence due to commence the next day.

Using Caution When Assessing Violence Potential

School personnel are encouraged to use the TOADS scheme to derive a preliminary estimation of an individual's violence potential. There is a certain risk that highly sensitive, well-meaning individuals may read too much into a situation and misidentify nonviolent students as being potentially violent. However, it should be noted that when there is a concern, accurate assessment of a subject's lethality risk must be conducted by individuals who have extensive hands-on experience and demonstrated expertise in making such evaluations. When children and others are facing the threat of death or severe assault, exhaustive efforts should be made to seek out the most qualified personnel. In cases where there is less clarity about the potential for violence, the following principles should be considered to help ensure that early warning signs are not misinterpreted:

1. Warning signs should never be used for stereotyping, which can harm an at-risk youth. In the aftermath of the Columbine tragedy there was concern that any students wearing black trench coats would be accused of somehow participating in the attack, just because Eric Harris and Dylan Klebold had been part of the "Trench Coat Mafia."

2. Behaviors need to be interpreted within a situational and developmental context. A threat made by a 5-year-old is often very different from a threat made by a 15-year-old. When documenting threats, it is important to place them in the context of the conversation or situation within which they occurred. A threat by a football player to "kill those guys" when referring to the opposing team is very different from the threats discussed throughout this book.

3. Perpetrators of schoolplace violence usually exhibit multiple warning signs, repeated over time, and with increased intensity and frequency. It is therefore important not to overreact to isolated signs that may portend nothing at all.

More Predictors: Pathways to Violence

In all of the previously mentioned cases of both workplace and schoolplace violence, the pathways to violence have been similar. The series of precipitating events has contained certain loosely recognizable phases. Not all of the perpetrators experienced all of these phases, and some may have escalated to violence so quickly that it is difficult to determine these substages; however, many of the schoolplace and workplace perpetrators go through this pathway to violence. Most perpetrators of both kinds of violence have experienced a perceived injustice, have already attempted resolution, have entertained violent fantasies and made some practice attempts, and have become confused about the distinction between fantasy and reality.

Step One: Perceived Injustice

First, for most perpetrators, there has been a string of perceived injustices ending with some form of rejection or discipline. A girlfriend has ended a relationship, an authority figure has doled out discipline, or peers have taunted the perpetrator. Sometimes the injustice is reality-based and would be upsetting to almost anyone. Many of the school-place perpetrators were victims of cruel bullying and harassment. Other times the perceived injustice will seem to outside observers to have been blown significantly out of proportion.

Harris and Klebold viewed themselves as victims of a high school hierarchy with jocks at the top and noncomformists like themselves at the bottom. Like many of their fellow perpetrators, they defined themselves as outsiders and as victims of an unfair class system within the ranks of the school. Like many other perpetrators of schoolplace violence, they were taunted by their more powerful peers and called names such as "dirtbag" and "faggot." They saw no other effective means of seeking revenge against these intolerable injustices than violence. The significant part of this characterization is that this is *their perspective*. More than one person has pointed out the irony in their self–perception as underprivileged victims when they came from middle- and upper–middle–class professional families. One of the assailants drove a BMW to school.

Bullying

While it is beyond the scope of this book to fully address the issues of bullying (see the list of resources in the back of this book), the fact remains that bullying appears to be a factor contributing to feelings of injustice on the part of many perpetrators. The *Journal of the American Medical Association* stresses that an effort to address bullying must be an important component of any attempt at violence prevention (Spivak & Prothrow–Stith, 2001). Research cited by the National Association of Secondary School Principals states that bullies and their victims are more prone to violent behavior, especially as they get older, than are those peers who are not associated with such behavior (Ballard, Argus, & Remley, 1999).

Many of the school shooters have been described as victims of cruel bullying by others. For instance, Andy Williams, the boy who killed two and wounded 13 in Santana, California, was ruthlessly teased. He was called a "freak," a "dork," and a "nerd" and was mocked for his small size.

Bullying has been defined in the *Journal of Educational Research* as a "form of aggressive behavior with an imbalance of power, [in which] the dominant person(s) intentionally and repeatedly cause distress by tormenting or harassing another less dominant person(s)" (Atlas & Pepler, 1998, p. 86). Bullying can be direct (physical attacks, intimidation, name–calling), or it can be indirect (nasty gossip, ostracism). In many cases large groups of peers are present during bullying episodes and very few make any attempt to stop it. Bullies often interpret the non–intervention of peers as a tacit sign of approval that gives the bully even more power.

Bullying is a common problem at schools. In a recent study conducted by the Kaiser Family Foundation ("Children Say," 2001), 74% of 8- to 11–year–olds said teasing and bullying occur at their school. This figure rose to 86% among children aged 12 to 15. This problem was rated as more common than smoking, drinking, drugs, or sex.

After the tragedy at Columbine, Colorado Attorney General Ken Salazar visited schools across his state and was amazed to discover that 5% of students stay home one or more days every month out of fear of bully attacks ("Many Colorado Students," 2000). Spurred by this assessment, the state's governor, Bill Owens, signed into law a bill aimed at preventing bullying in schools.

Step Two: Attempted Resolution

The perpetrator's next step is to initiate a resolution. The perpetrator may initially attempt to resolve the matter through appropriate channels, without getting the desired results. For workplace violence situations at step two, the perpetrator may file grievances or complaints with supervisors. In schoolplace violence situations, perpetrators may try to distance themselves from those who are causing them irritation. When their efforts don't produce results, instead of dropping the issue these perpetrators become obsessed with it and move into the third phase.

Step Three: Violent Fantasies

During the third phase, problem solving narrows and the perpetrator begins to create violent fantasies of retaliation. These fantasies become very satisfying to the avenger, who can rework and replay the scene to play out as desired. The details of these images interest the perpetrator— who is there, how are they responding, where do they go? Sometimes these fantasies are fueled by knowledge of other schoolplace shootings that have taken place in the recent past. Other fantasies are augmented by song lyrics and by stories from movies, television, or books.

Step Four: Fantasy Becomes Reality

When the satisfaction from the fantasies begins to wane, avengers will start to act on their ideas. They may begin with low–level forms of violence such as graffiti, morbid writing, or threats. We call this type of behavior *practice sessions*, and elaborate on this concept in chapter 5.

Without confrontation, avengers will escalate behavior to more dangerous levels. Avengers may have specific targets in mind, or they may be angry at the world. In their violent rampage they may not hesitate to hurt as many people as possible because they are often suicidal and consider the shooting to be their legacy, their final statement.

Creating Barriers

In discussing violence prevention and intervention, it may be useful to think of the violent individual as a skier. As perpetrators start down the "hill" of becoming violent, most tend to start slowly and build up speed. Sometimes they start with low-level threats or vandalism to test out how the system will respond. They continue to escalate until they hit a barrier in their path.

Questioning can be an effective barrier. Sometimes the investigation process is enough deterrence. Confronting ups the ante. A warning is a confrontation barrier. A security system is a confrontation barrier, as is a police barricade. The next level of barrier involves implementing consequences. A range of consequences exists, from probation to community service to suspension or expulsion. Legal consequences are also an option. Once the perpetrators hit a barrier, they have an opportunity to rethink their plan. At this point they may consider backing off. In less happy scenarios they may simply choose to go around the barrier and go on about their business.

Perpetrators can see some barriers from quite a distance away and will avoid them. Some barriers are easily identified as mirages—nothing real at all, just a symbol for others to see. Perpetrators sail right through these barriers. But effective barriers are so large that perpetrators know they will not get around them, so perpetrators stop on their own. For those perpetrators determined to get down the hill, protectors must plant many barriers to slow the rate of descent. In the chapters that follow we offer many suggestions to guide those who wish to create barriers that will slow or stop potential perpetrators of schoolplace violence.

One-Way Ticket

Setting up barriers to violence is a one-way ticket. Once you have implemented an intervention, you cannot go backwards. As mentioned earlier, there have been defining events that change the fabric of our culture forever—razor blades in Halloween treats, product tampering, and, all too recently, airline terrorists. These events cause "fence posts" to be put in place. That is, protective action is taken. Once the fence posts go up, they cannot come down. It would be hard to imagine aspirin bottles today without tamper–resistant seals, or airline travel without the new searches and x–raying of luggage.

Over time, security measures become safety signals. People see an armed guard at a bank and feel confident that robbers will choose to go elsewhere. Most people feel insecure when driving a car without a seat belt fastened, even if it is just across a parking lot. Effective security measures provide a barrier between a potential victim and perpetrator, but none can guarantee safety. Nevertheless, once a fence post goes up, it stays up.

Part II

Interrupting Schoolplace Violence

Chapter Three

Near Misses:
Secrets of School Violence

The most kept secret about schoolplace violence is this: *Not all would-be perpetrators succeed in pulling off their plans.* We are misled by media concentration on only those events that end in tragedy. Less attention—often no attention—is paid to near misses, foiled plots to initiate school violence. This is a shame, because near misses offer us a blueprint for prevention efforts. We have much to learn from thwarted violence. Near misses teach us about the warning signs of potential violence. Near misses help us learn to gauge the seriousness of threats. Near misses provide answers to a number of crucial questions: Why were some situations successfully interrupted while others were not? Who stepped in to stop the violence? How did they step in—what action was taken? How did they know what was about to happen? Answering such questions about cases where violence was averted can guide us in building more effective prevention plans.

One of the biggest and most heartening lessons learned since the tragedy at Columbine is that *even when all the factors predictive of violence are present in a given situation, the violent act can be successfully interrupted.* Since April 20, 1999, there have been at least 35 major documented plans for schoolplace violence. However, only 13 of those cases ended in actual violence. The other 22 were successfully interrupted *before* violence occurred. What was common to all successfully interrupted cases was that people—usually students—who heard threats took them seriously and reported them to the appropriate authorities—usually parents, school officials, or law enforcement. In turn, the parents, school administration, and law enforcement personnel took the reports seriously and thoroughly investigated the students in question. In other words, these people put in place at least two of the previously mentioned barriers: *questioning* and *confronting.*

Detection of Near Misses

Following are summaries of some of the major incidents of potential schoolplace violence that were successfully interrupted. Detailed here are what signs were present, who made the report, how people responded to the report, and what was found after the report was investigated.

May 13, 1999: Port Huron, Michigan

Jedaiah Zinzo and Justin Schnepp were both 14 years old. Together they constructed a plan to outdo the Columbine shootings by first arming themselves and then forcing the principal of Holland Woods Middle School to call an assembly where the two boys could begin killing teachers, classmates, and, ultimately, themselves. Zinzo and Schnepp had made a list of 154 targets, had stolen a blueprint of the school from the custodian's office, and had plotted to use one gun to steal more. Zinzo's and Schnepp's classmates learned of their plan and reported it to the assistant principal. After a police investigation, Zinzo and Schnepp were sentenced to 4 years probation.

May 19, 1999: Anaheim, California

A student at South Junior High heard that a couple of other boys were threatening to blow up the school. He decided to notify the police who then conducted searches of the two eighth graders' homes. The police recovered bombs, bomb-making materials, a military-surplus rifle, a Ruger Blackhawk .45-caliber handgun, 1,500 rounds of ammunition, and Nazi paraphernalia.

August 24, 1999: Palatka, Florida

William Black, age 17, and Jeffrey Carter, age 16, were arrested after their history teacher discovered in their possession a drawing depicting dead students and a student with a bloody knife, a shotgun, and an assault weapon. When the teacher questioned Carter about the drawing, Carter said he and Black intended to outdo the tragedy at Columbine. The boys admitted to their teacher that they were outcasts because they worshipped Satan. The teacher then reported this discussion to the school resource officer and the principal. The students then claimed they made up the story to get the teacher upset. The authorities were not deterred. They arrested the students and turned them over to the Department of Juvenile Justice.

October 28, 1999: Cleveland, Ohio

Adam Gruber, age 14, John Borowski, age 15, Benjamin Balducci, age 16, and Andy Napier, age 15, were white students attending a mostly African American school. They planned an attack on the school that was supposed to end in a suicidal shoot-out with the police. Police and school officials were notified about the boys' plan by a parent of another student attending the school. A police investigation uncovered guns, maps, and a recruit list. Arrests were made in the case and charges were filed against the boys.

May 18, 2000: Millbrae, California

At first the other students were too scared to report the threats made by a 17-year-old senior at Mills High School. When one student did finally come forward after another student reported being threatened with a gun, the would-be perpetrator was arrested. A police investigation uncovered an arsenal of 15 guns and rifles, plus knives and ammunition, all kept at the boy's home. During the 8 months prior to this incident, the student had often boasted that he was going to "do a Columbine" at school.

February 5, 2001: Hoyt, Kansas

On the basis of a call made to an anonymous tip line by a student, police began investigating high school students Richard B. Bradley Jr., age 18, Jason L. Moss, age 17, and James R. Lopez, age 16. The tipster was concerned because the suspects were building and detonating bombs. The police discovered bomb-making material, hand-drawn floor plans of Royal Valley High School, a rifle, ammunition, and white supremacist drawings in the boys' homes. Police also recovered three black trench coats similar to those worn by the Columbine High School gunmen. The students were arrested and charges were filed.

February 7, 2001: Fort Collins, Colorado

Three boys at Preston Jr. High School—Alexander Vukodinovich, age 14, Chad Meiniger, age 15, and Scott Parent, age 14—were planning to "redo Columbine" at their school. Eventually, after the three boys threatened to kill them, too, two female classmates of the boys notified police and their parents about the plans. A police investigation recovered a weapons cache, ammunition, and sketches of the school. The boys were arrested.

February 11, 2001: Palm Harbor, Florida

Scott McClain, age 14, wrote a detailed e-mail to at least one friend describing his plans to make a bomb and possibly target a specific teacher at Palm Harbor Middle School. The friend's mother alerted law enforcement. McClain was arrested. When police searched McClain's home they found a partially assembled bomb that would have had a "kill radius" of 15 feet.

February 14, 2001: Elmira, New York

Jeremy Getman, age 18 and a senior at Southside High School, passed a disturbing note to a friend. The friend then alerted the authorities about the content of the note. Police found Getman in Southside High School's cafeteria with a .22-caliber Ruger semiautomatic and a duffel bag containing 18 bombs and a sawed-off shotgun. He was arrested. Further investigation recovered eight more bombs in Getman's home.

March 7, 2001: Twentynine Palms, California

Two 17-year-old boys from Monument High School were arrested on suspicion of conspiracy to commit murder and civil rights violations. This was because a female student had overheard the boys' plans for violence and notified police. The police investigated the report and recovered a rifle and a list consisting of 16 individuals who the boys had intended to kill. Charges were filed.

Note that in almost every case reported here, barriers prevented potential violence from becoming actual. Threats were not ignored; they were reported. Reports were not ignored, they were followed up with questioning and various kinds of police activity, mainly in the form of investigations and searches, a very strong form of confrontation indeed. In almost every case consequences were implemented in the form of arrests and the filing of charges.

The data available suggest that most threats of violence were interrupted because would-be perpetrators boasted about their intentions, threatened to do harm, or spoke of their plans loudly enough so they could be overheard. The perpetrators were either sending threatening e-mails or letters, verbally announcing their intentions in the presence of others, or telling friends about what they planned to do. Regardless of the mode of communication, in all of the incidents at least one person knew something about there being a potential for violence. This information was then reported, sometimes through parents, either to authorities within the school or to law enforcement. It appears that one of the greatest lessons learned from the tragedy at Columbine, and from those events that could have but did not occur, is the importance of responding to warning signs and threats of potential school violence.

Such a response was seen in Wheeling, Illinois. Nine days after the tragedy at Columbine, a ninth-grade boy was arrested for indirectly threatening to do harm to his school. This boy was described as an "unpopular nerd" and was often ridiculed for the way he dressed. At lunch a group of kids approached him and said that he was a lot like Harris and Klebold. The boy responded, "I could be." These words, as simple as they seemed, launched a very appropriate response by authorities. The boy's locker was searched and a baseball bat found inside it. The boy was charged with disorderly conduct for making a threat and having a weapon in his locker, and spent 6 months in counseling. He was then transferred to another school where he is reportedly doing very well. Although some may feel that the reaction to the boy's statement was exaggerated, it is difficult to know what he might have done if the situation had been left unchecked.

This is perhaps the most difficult aspect of successfully interrupting schoolplace violence: the uncertainty. When an interruption occurs, it is hard to know exactly what actions were stopped. Students, parents, law enforcement, and teachers will know that they did not do enough only when it is already too late.

The responsibility for recognizing and reporting danger signs does not fall only on those directly related to the school system. It falls also on people in the community. A prime example is in the case of Al Joseph DeGuzman, a college sophomore in Cupertino, California. DeGuzman idolized the gunmen from Columbine High School and was planning to shoot up and bomb his community college in January 2001. His plan was interrupted, however, by the report of a store clerk. DeGuzman had taken pictures of himself with his arsenal of weapons and pipe bombs. When he had them developed the store clerk took notice and contacted the police. Had the store clerk not acted on her suspicions, DeAnza College in Cupertino could have been another figure in the statistics on schoolplace violence. When police investigated DeGuzman's home, they found the arsenal, a sketch of the campus, a timeline for an attack, and an audiotape containing an apology. The mass murder was supposed to occur at 12:30 p.m. Police discovered his arsenal packed and ready to go only 10 hours before (Foo & Vasquez, 2001).

The Copycat Phenomenon

As people become more aware of the need to detect potential violence and report it to a centralized group of authorities—what we are calling a *communication vortex*—who can investigate the threat, they are also becoming more aware of the similarities that exist between the various incidents of schoolplace violence both interrupted and completed. The incidents tend to resemble one another. This is true because children are extremely susceptible to the influences of social learning. Adolescents seem especially predisposed to mimic behaviors that are highly visible, and such behaviors, it turns out, can include innovative means of destruction.

This means that the copycat phenomenon is especially prevalent within this 11–21 age group, and is a potentially lethal learning tool. As one student remarked in the aftermath of the Springfield, Oregon, massacre, "It's a copycat thing. You watch a cooking show and learn how to cook. You watch the news and learn how to kill."

During the 4 weeks following the tragedy at Columbine, more than 350 students were arrested on charges related to violent threats against schools. Two days after the shootings at Santana High School, in Santee, California, in which a 15-year-old boy killed two and wounded 13 others, at least 13 other students in California were arrested and several more were suspended for allegedly making threats against classmates or bringing weapons to school (Groves & Krikorian, 2001). These numbers further support the notion that people are becoming more responsive to threats of violence and are successfully preventing new plans of violence from coming to fruition.

While not all of the following are confirmed copycat crimes, the patterns are striking:

- In January 1993, Scott Pennington held his class hostage in Grayson, Kentucky. Less than a year and a half later, Clay Shrout held his high school class hostage in Union, Kentucky. Each used his father's pistols.

- On November 15, 1995, Jamie Rouse killed one teacher and one student at Richland High. Shortly after, Jamie's younger brother Jeremy was convicted of solicitation to commit murder when he tried to recruit friends to "finish the job" his brother started. Jeremy stated that he was angry that some students said he cheered on his brother and could have prevented the shootings. Jeremy spent 2 years in the custody of a juvenile facility.

- On December 15, 1997, Colt Todd of Stamps, Arkansas, shot students from the perimeter of school grounds as they entered school. Fifteen months later two boys in Jonesboro, Arkansas, shot their classmates from the woods near their school.

- Loukaitis, Kinkel, Harris, and Klebold all wore dark trench coats.

- Carneal and Loukaitis had both read Stephen King's novel *Rage*. In the story, a boy takes his class hostage and murders his teacher. King wrote the book under the pseudonym Richard Bachman during his own difficult teenage years. King said that he recalled "the feeling of rejection, of being an outsider, what it was like to be teased relentlessly, and to entertain the visions, fantasies of revenge on the people who'd done it to you" (Hall, 1998). King has since taken the book out of print because of the story's resemblance to instances of school shootings (Walker, 1999).

Immediately after the Columbine shootings there were countless threats of bombs and killing sprees made by students in the Denver metro area, as well as around the country. Three days after the tragedy at Columbine, five junior high school students in Texas were charged with conspiring to kill students and teachers at Danforth Junior High School. As many as 30 youths in the state of Texas were investigated, held for questioning, or charged with suspicion of plans for school violence involving an alleged bomb plot. A search of the suspects' homes revealed crude explosive devices, gunpowder, and Internet documents with instructions on bomb-making.

In Taber, Alberta, Canada, on Wednesday, April 25, 1999, shots were fired in the hallway at W. R. Myers High School. A 17-year-old boy was killed and another was seriously wounded. A 14-year-old former student, who had been expelled from school for setting off a smoke bomb, entered the school with a sawed-off rifle under a long parka. The student was known by his peers as someone who was "freaky" and unpopular (Pritchett, 1999).

In Colorado, copycat behaviors incessantly threatened schools. Two weeks after the Columbine shootings, four teens plotted a copycat attack on Adams City High School. An informant provided written plans, detailed drawings, and a map of the building, all allegedly assembled by the teens (Miniclier & Robinson, 1999). A Kennedy High School student was arrested when his plot to blow up the school was exposed. As in the Columbine shootings, he created a "hit list" of students he was planning to kill. A Denver police officer said the youth told him "it would be Columbine all over again" (Robinson & Chronis, 1999).

One month to the day after the tragedy at Columbine, a 15-year-old boy brought two guns to a suburban high school near Atlanta and injured six students. His friends described him as a "gun lover" who was crushed by a recent romantic breakup. Since that time many more cases of completed and interrupted school violence have been attempts to mimic the Columbine shootings, including cases in California, Colorado, Kansas, Florida, and Ohio. In all of these cases, the links to the tragedy at Columbine and previous schoolplace violence incidents provide clear evidence of the copycat phenomenon.

Thus, when schools are looking to interrupt this form of violence, they should be keenly aware when a school violence incident makes local, national, and international headlines. This news becomes a triggering event. When this occurs, schools should reassess their high-risk students.

Chapter Four

Developing Policies and Procedures

Protectors will never know if they have overreacted, they will only know if they have underreacted. In other words, if protectors take precautions and violence never occurs, they will never know—was prevention effective or was violence never going to occur in the first place?

Many schools are developing standard operating guides to help them navigate violence prevention, and we will explore some tips on developing these guides in this chapter, but first, some words of caution. There are no cookie-cutter approaches to violence prevention. What may work in one school may be inappropriate with another school's culture and dynamics. Each school must be willing to adapt and experiment with the suggestions to make them fit with the school's unique needs and concerns. Second, there are no foolproof formulas for preventing violence. For instance, concerned teachers identified Kip Kinkel as a youth at risk for violence. His parents were involved in attempting to discipline him and get him the treatment he needed. He had been taking Prozac and had attended anger-management counseling. When people are 100% determined to carry out an act of violence, they will find a way. Fortunately, most violent individuals, like most suicidal individuals, harbor some degree of ambivalence. The more effective the preventive measures that are in place, the greater the likelihood that violence will be deterred because that ambivalence will be met with barriers—confrontation and consequences.

Between Pollyanna and Paranoia

The thought that a violent massacre could occur at one's school is so distressing that many people respond in one of two extreme ways that we might characterize as Pollyanna or paranoia. Pollyanna responders see the world through rose-colored glasses. They believe in the inherent goodness of people and want to instill values of open-mindedness and acceptance. These responders are likely to believe that if they avoid talking about violent incidents at other schools, everyone will forget and history will not repeat itself. This approach creates a likelihood that people will naively enter dangerous situations without the awareness or skills to keep themselves safe. By contrast, paranoid responders are overly sensitive to the dangers of the world, and would prefer to keep schools in a lockdown mode. Individuals under the guidance of these paranoid types are apt to rebel against the precautions, or become immobilized with fear.

People should be able to talk about violence in a realistic and balanced way. Given today's apparent trend toward increased violence, violence prevention is as important as fire prevention or other disaster preparedness. Most people do not think that disaster preparedness is overreactive or destructive. Each school community will need to decide where they fall on the continuum from Pollyanna to paranoia and respond with interventions that best fit their culture. The prevention and intervention strategies listed below can serve as a starting place for schools developing a standard operating guide to help them avoid and respond to schoolplace violence.

Legal Considerations

While it is outside the scope of this book to give legal advice, there are some issues that we encourage schools to consider as they are drafting their policies. Very often schools are faced with legal concerns from both sides of a decision. They risk being either negligent or wrongfully accusatory. At this point, they must decide what type of lawsuit they would rather face (Nicoletti, Spencer-Thomas, & Bollinger, 2001).

School Boundaries and Scope of Responsibilities

When people think about a school campus, they often think about the physical grounds. But the boundaries of a campus are diffuse and permeable. "School violence" can involve visitors on school grounds, students at an off-campus field trip, even individuals passing through school property. Do the school boundaries include the sidewalks and other areas adjacent to the school property? For what situations are schools potentially liable? Where do schools draw the line in terms of taking responsibility for preventing violence? These are some of the questions that each school, along with its legal counsel, must consider.

And what about student behavior that diverges from the established code of conduct, but occurs during a spring break or summer vacation? What happens if a student is charged with a serious crime, but is awaiting trial? Should the school temporarily suspend the student or wait until the courts decide guilt or innocence? These are all difficult questions with which schools have just begun to wrestle.

Failure to Protect/Failure to Warn

When a school tries to control or prohibit dangerous behavior such as bullying or violent threats, a court may find that the institution has a duty to protect the potential victims. Suits against schools can result in monetary awards for damages such as failure to provide adequate security or prevent foreseeable harm.

Liability of Schools for Wrongful Accusations and Discharge

School authorities must be able to handle threats and violent behavior in a way that protects individuals from defamation of character. The International Association of Chiefs of Police (IACP) advises that this form of liability can be minimized by conducting prompt investigations of all allegations and by notifying only those people who have a need to know. Any dismissal of employees or students must be consistent with the laws and appropriate to the behavior.

Violation of Students' Rights

All search and seizure policies should be consistent with the Fourth Amendment to the Constitution as well as local and state statutes (IACP,

2001). For instance, one must have a reasonable suspicion that a law or school rule has been violated based on reliable information, proven facts, or known circumstances. There must be an appropriate relationship between the severity of the threat and the degree of intrusiveness of any search conducted. School authorities also must keep in mind that students have a right to due process before being suspended or expelled. Finally, students have rights to privacy when it comes to record keeping and information sharing. School authorities must be sure to be in compliance with all applicable laws pertaining to confidentiality. (See the section on documentation for a further exploration of confidentiality.)

On behalf of six students, the American Civil Liberties Union (ACLU) is suing a high school in Los Angeles for unconstitutional search and seizure procedures. These students claim that they were patted down in front of the blackboard and were never told why they were being searched ("California School Sued," 2001).

Currently, there is a case before the Ninth U.S. Circuit Court of Appeals that is wrestling with the First Amendment rights. The central issue in the case is whether writing violent poems for class is a school risk worthy of suspension or a right of free speech. In 1998, a 16-year-old wrote a poem called "Last Words," which included such violent phrases as "I drew my gun and Bang, Bang, Bang–Bang. When it was all over, 28 were dead" ("School Suspension," 2001).

Development of a Threat and Violence Assessment Team

The first step in addressing violence prevention is the development of a Threat and Violence Assessment Team (TVAT). As the National School Safety Center (1999) notes, "School safety is a community concern requiring a community response." This team should consist of individuals trained in the evaluation of, and intervention with, potentially violent situations. Other specialties that would benefit the team are policy development, media and public relations, human relations, and fund-raising. While building this coalition, schools should be selective in choosing representatives. Solution seekers should be favored over status seekers. The group's objective is violence prevention and response. Potential team members include the following:

- Principal

- Teachers

- Local law enforcement/School resource officers

- Legal advisors

- Students

- Parents

- School security officers

- School psychologists

- Professional violence consultant

The Threat and Violence Assessment Team is responsible for making critical decisions quickly. They will develop the protocol for response in case of a threat or violent incident. Other responsibilities include

- Evaluating potential violence problems

- Assessing individual students' potential for violence

- Selecting intervention techniques

- Establishing a plan for the protection of students, staff, and other potential targets

- Coordinating with affected parties such as victims, families, employees, media, government, or law enforcement/rescue personnel

- Knowing about victim assistance and community service programs

- Assisting with placement in immediate and ongoing counseling resources

The team must work in conjunction with local law enforcement to prevent guesswork in times of crisis. Authority and autonomy issues must be determined in advance. Specifically, when a school is in a siege situation, law enforcement officials should be the incident commanders and assume authority. The scope of the other responsibilities of the group and particular individuals' tasks should be assigned.

Policy Development

According to Ronald Stephens of the National School Safety Center, "good policies prevent problems before they occur and can help mitigate problems once they emerge. Good policies can also preclude a series of successive problems which might otherwise occur in the absence of appropriate policies" (Stephens, 1995, p. 57). Policies reduce the chance factors in school operations by establishing a common body of knowledge. Schools that develop a "Standard Operating Guide" before it is needed are more likely to avoid panic and disruption when an event arises. Research supported by the National Institute of Justice has demonstrated that policies are most effective when they are grounded in research drawing from diverse disciplines ("Preventing School Violence," n.d.).

The National School Boards Association (1999) recommends that those developing policies to prevent violence in schools consider a specific series of questions:

- Is the content of the policy within the scope of the board's authority?

- Is it consistent with local, state, and federal laws?

- Have legal references been included?

- Does it reflect good educational practice?

- Is it reasonable? (Are any requirements or prohibitions arbitrary or discriminatory?)

- Does it adequately cover the issue?

- Is it limited to one policy topic?

- Is it cross-referenced to other relevant policy topics?

- Is it consistent with the board's existing policies?

- Can it be administered?

- Is it practical in terms of administrative enforcement and budget?

The following sections on policy development have been adapted from *Violence Goes to Work: An Employer's Guide* (Denver, CO: Mountain States Employers Council & Nicoletti-Flater Associates, 1997).

Who Develops Policies?

A violence prevention policy is most effective when it is created, implemented, and managed by those who are directly involved with such matters on a regular basis. A cross section of the prevention community should be involved to get varying viewpoints on the policy strategies. As always, legal counsel should be sought before any policies are put into practice.

What Policies Are Necessary?

Most schools have an expected code of conduct for their students, but this is only the first step in developing necessary policies for preventing violence. Other important considerations include how to handle threats, searches, reporting, investigation, response, crisis management, and violence aftermath. Some of these issues will be covered here, while others can be found in their respective chapters.

Threat Policy

Create a written zero–tolerance policy (see chapter 6 for our definition of zero tolerance) that explains the position of the school on intimidating, threatening, or violent behaviors. Clearly define what constitutes a threat (see chapter 5). Include only policy criteria that can be administered consistently. Key elements include the following:

- Commitment from upper–level school administrators to develop and enforce the policy.

- Training for teachers in identifying and defusing problems and conflicts.

- Training for students in identifying and reporting threats.

- A strong statement by the school district prohibiting intimidation, threats, weapons, and violence on school property.

- Written communication to all students and school employees about the district's policy on reporting procedures. An avenue for anonymous reporting should be provided, but language that guarantees strict confidentiality for reporting should be avoided.

- A policy that does not promise to protect students or employees from physical harm, because this is not absolutely possible. It is preferable to claim that the school will "strive" to promote and maintain an environment free from intimidation and threats of violence.

- A decision regarding the use of "may" and "will" in the text of the policy. The use of the word "will" can be a promise to act. If a complaint is received and NOT investigated, the school district could face a negligence claim.

- Specified consequences for violation of the threat policy (e.g., police report, suspension/expulsion, counseling, community service).

- Mention of the degree to which parents will be involved in the intervention. A parent conference can help communicate concerns and investigate other questionable behaviors.

The sample policies on page 71 incorporate some of the features emphasized above. Policies should be developed with suggestions from individuals who view students from a multitude of perspectives and in a variety of situations. This well-rounded approach offers the opportunity to catch the early warning signs while there is still time for effective intervention.

According to Ronald Stephens (1995), the following are additional areas to consider when developing a comprehensive school policy on violence prevention:

- Alternative activities for young people

- Collaboration with other agencies

- Crime-free school zones

- Student conduct/discipline code

- Emergency preparedness

- Home-school linkages (e.g., parent skills training, volunteer parent patrols)

Sample Threat and Violence Policy

Our policy is to strive to maintain a school environment free from intimidation, threats, or violent acts. Prohibited behavior includes, but is not limited to intimidating, threatening, or hostile behaviors; physical abuse; vandalism; arson; sabotage; carrying or use of weapons; or any other act that, in the administration's opinion, is inappropriate to the school environment. In addition, bizarre or offensive comments regarding violent events and/or aggressive behaviors will not be tolerated.

School employees or students who feel subjected to any of the behaviors listed above should immediately report the incident to _____ [name of designated school representative(s)]. All complaints will receive prompt attention and the situation will be investigated. Based on the results of the inquiry, disciplinary action that the administration feels is appropriate will be taken.

School employees or students who observe or have knowledge of violation of this policy should immediately report it to _____ [the appointed school representative(s)]. We will investigate these events and will request the cooperation of all incident-related individuals. An employee or student who believes there is a serious threat to the safety and health of others should report this concern directly to law enforcement authorities.

Sample Search Policy

As a school district, we reserve the right to conduct at any time, without notice, searches and inspections of students' personal effects, as well as of school-issued property. Searchable items may include, but will not be limited to, lunch boxes, thermoses, purses, lockers, desks, computers (e-mail, Web pages, and files), backpacks, sports equipment and bags, and packages brought onto school property.

Any illegal, dangerous, or unauthorized articles discovered may be taken into custody and may be turned over to law enforcement representatives. Any student who refuses to submit property for inspection, or who is found in possession of prohibited articles or items, will be subjected to disciplinary action, up to and including expulsion from the school district.

Source: Adapted from Mountain States Employers Council & Nicoletti-Flater Associates (1997). *Violence Goes to Work*. MSEC & NFA.

- Search and seizure issues

- Security personnel in schools

- Specialized curriculum and/or training

- Weapons in school

While not all of these topics are within the scope of this manual, they are adequately covered in other resources listed in the references and additional resources sections.

Investigation of Threats and Violent Incidents

This section has been developed from *Violence Goes to Work: An Employer's Guide* (Denver, CO: Mountain States Employers Council & Nicoletti–Flater Associates, 1997) and "Threat Assessment: An Approach to Prevent Targeted Violence" by R. Fein and B. Vossekuil (*National Institute of Justice: Research in Action,* Washington, DC: U.S. Department of Justice, 1995, July).

A formalized plan for investigation of threats or violence complaints is necessary to prevent school personnel from being caught off guard and unprepared when a prompt response is most critical. A carefully thought–out investigation procedure helps ensure that facts about the incident are collected and examined in an expedient, methodical, and thorough manner. Multiple sources of information are essential in learning about a person's behavior, interests, and motivation at various times. One question to keep in mind during the investigation process is this: What might change in the perpetrator's life that might increase or decrease the risk for violence?

The investigator should also gather information about the potential target(s). Are they identifiable and vulnerable to attack? Is the target afraid, and is this fear shared by others? How sophisticated or naive is the target in assessing safety?

During the initial stages of the investigation, witnesses may be reluctant to come forward for fear of reprisal or lack of action on the part of school or law enforcement authorities. Schools need to reassure witnesses that they will do all they can to provide protection and intervene appropriately.

Security measures for intended victims and other witnesses must be taken seriously. Security should center on *target hardening*—making these targets less accessible. Agencies can sometimes be remiss in making these efforts effective and instead apply only "window dressing" efforts. After Columbine, visitors to the school were required to sign in and wear a sticker badge. This effort is not an effective deterrent for most perpetrators, especially students who are already part of the school culture.

Investigators can also be thrown off track by perpetrators who tend to minimize and compartmentalize their actions. "I was just joking" or "the statement was taken out of context" are common excuses that they use. They have a story for everything. Their stories can distract investigators from seeing the patterns over time.

Parents can be important witnesses as well as difficult obstacles in an investigation. They may try to protect, minimize, and rationalize. And they may sue. Therefore, it is critical to bring parents into the process of the investigation as team members as early as possible.

A rapid response is essential when threats are made. We were called in to consult on a case where a student had written threatening notes at school. The incident was reported to the principal who called the Mental Health Team in to evaluate the threats. From our recommendations, students and teachers were interviewed and law officials were able to locate a gun very quickly.

Who Conducts the Investigation?

The individual(s) appointed to analyze the situation should have training in schoolplace violence. They must keep a neutral and objective attitude toward all parties and have the ability to manage the investigation in a professional manner. At various points, the administration may wish to use outside experts who have knowledge and experience in evidence collection and in conducting investigations, interviews, and interrogations. An alternative is to designate appropriately trained members of the Threat and Violence Assessment Team to conduct the investigation. A series of steps that involve planning, conducting, documenting, and evaluating the investigation is necessary for an effective, thorough analysis of the evidence.

Plan the Investigation

Investigations of school violence can take years—especially when the scope of the violence reaches the magnitude of the events at Columbine. There have been three separate investigations of the Littleton tragedy, and several suits are still pending. Investigations are challenging because emotions run high and people want immediate answers. Investigators often learn the hard way how to manage the families' right to privacy and the public's right to know. Several pieces of evidence, including autopsy and crime scene images from Columbine, made their way into the media, adding significant distress to the grieving families.

Investigators may also become frustrated by the way evidence is collected. In the case of Columbine, mental health records were never released, and journals and computer data were not turned over to a central location in a timely manner so that definitive action could be taken. Some critical pieces of evidence in the Columbine case included the following:

- The infamous "basement tapes" that showed Harris and Klebold describing their action plan
- Class projects referring to the students' violent interests
- Web sites frequented by Harris and Klebold
- The students' musical interests
- Comments they made in classes and to peers

Draft investigation procedures prior to conducting any actual investigation. Consistent and comprehensive inquiries result when a detailed methodology is followed in each case. Throughout the investigation process you are looking for behavioral data that gives evidence for motivation, intention, and capacity to commit violence. Types of data needed include these:

- Interviews with the person or persons in question
- Journals, letters, books, and magazines related to the investigation
- Collateral interviews with family members, friends, coworkers, supervisors, and neighbors

- Police and court records

- Mental health records

- Computer histories—Web sites visited, e-mails, online profiles

- Armament inventories

- School records—discipline and grades

Steps in the Investigation Process

- Step 1: Develop a preliminary list of witnesses or individuals involved in, or affected by, the incident.

- Step 2: Specify the sequence of interviews and appoint interviewers.

- Step 3: Determine what evidence the investigator can obtain for the investigation.

- Step 4: Decide what, if any, action is necessary before beginning the investigation. For example, consider implementation of security measures to protect targets and/or property, or suspension of accused student(s) during the investigation.

Prepare for the Interview

Take into account aspects of the physical environment and ensure privacy for each interview. This is critical if students and employees are to feel free to discuss the problem.

- Determine the type of information needed from each person.

- Anticipate possible reactions or responses from the alleged perpetrator.

- Develop a list of questions in advance to ask each party. Contemplate the objective of the individual and what information is required.

- Establish rapport; remember to be empathetic and calm, because the victim may be in shock. Give the interviewee time to answer; do not be impatient.

- Direct questions to the matters related to the complaint or event, unless past patterns of this conduct have been identified, in which case this history is open to questioning.

- Develop questions concerning who, what, where, when, and how.

- Document what each party involved did, said, or knew.

- Follow appropriate questioning techniques:

  - Ask open-ended questions, encouraging the individual(s) to share more information.

  - Listen to the response without interrupting the flow of details.

  - Wait until the person has completed the narrative to ask for clarification.

  - Keep each question brief and confined to one point or topic.

  - Avoid leading questions that suggest or guide the answer.

  - Keep questions simple, using words that are clear to the person being interviewed.

  - Watch for nonverbal messages and follow up with applicable questions to confirm or revise the received impression.

Conduct the Interview

Begin the investigation with the individual who reported the occurrence. Ask for details: What happened? What action did each party take? What did each person say? Can you describe where the action took place? Then proceed to get answers to the questions listed below. After this initial interview is completed, ask the same questions of the individual named as behaving in an intimidating, threatening, or violent manner, and of any witnesses in an order appropriate to the situation. With witnesses or other involved parties, it is important to ask general questions first such as, "Are you aware of any problems that exist between students at our school?"

In all of these interviews you will be trying to elicit answers about the alleged perpetrator and his or her motivations. The kinds of questions you will want answered include

- Has the individual shown interest in other school violence incidents, school shooters, weapons, extremist groups, or murder?

- Has the individual engaged in attack–related behavior, including any menacing, harassing, or stalking–type behavior?

- Has the individual experienced a recent loss or loss of status?

- Is the person suicidal or experiencing feelings of desperation or despair?

- What motivated the individual to make the threatening statement or behavior?

- What has the individual communicated to anyone regarding his or her intentions?

- When did it happen? Get both the date and time of the incident.

- Who was present? List the names of any potential witnesses.

- What factors in the individual's life and/or environment might increase or decrease the likelihood that the individual would attempt to attack a target?

At the conclusion of the interview, ask for a written statement summarizing the incident.

(Adapted from International Association of Chiefs of Police [2001]. *Guide for Preventing and Responding to School Violence.* Alexandria, VA: Author.)

Document the Investigation

Prepare a confidential report of the investigation findings in case of a filed charge or lawsuit. The investigative notes and statements of witnesses may be used as an official record. Therefore, be sure there are no extraneous comments, statements, or opinions cited as fact. Stick to the objective, verifiable data of the event and do not embellish.

- Include all actual findings and their sources.

- Keep the report as confidential as is practical. Only those with a legitimate need to know should have access to the report. Make no copies unless necessary. Confidentiality should be waived, however, when a threat becomes imminent and potential victims need to be warned. In a case we evaluated, a student made a veiled threat about "taking care" of someone who would anger or upset him. We recommended that if he did make a more identifiable threat, he would lose his rights to confidentiality so that appropriate safety procedures could be put in place for any individuals named as targets.

- Avoid defamation claims. Defamation is the unprivileged communication to a third person of a false statement intending to harm the reputation of another. To protect against the possibility of defamation, make the findings of an investigation and other pertinent documents available only to persons having a legitimate connection to or interest in them. Do not give secretaries, supervisors, and other personnel not directly involved in the investigation access to any of the documents. Precautions against needless publication of potentially defamatory statements will minimize the exposure of the school to liability.

"A carefully and comprehensively documented record may be criticized for imperfect data–gathering or flawed analysis, but such a record also demonstrates both thoughtfulness and good faith—critical questions in any postincident review" (Fein & Vossekuil, 1995).

Evaluate the Evidence and Take Action

The investigating team has an obligation to analyze the data collected and formulate a course of action. This is especially difficult when the only information available is one person's word against another's. Consultation with an outside violence assessment professional is often needed in evaluating the evidence.

To consider the credibility of the allegations, ask the following questions:

- When was the complaint made? If it was not immediately reported, find out why.

- Is the complaint specific and detailed? Are there any contradictions in the information collected?

- Are there things missing in the evidence that should be there? Is there any logical explanation for the missing data?

To consider the credibility of the accused, and any denials, ask the following questions:

- Has the student accused simply made a blanket denial?

- Has the accused provided evidence that either supports or contradicts the allegations?

- Have other allegations been made about this person?

Once the evidence has been weighed, appropriate action should be taken in relation to the perpetrator, the potential victim(s), and the sense of security for the rest of the school community. For more suggestions on appropriate action, see chapter 6.

Chapter Five

Detection and Awareness

Myth #1: "He Just Snapped!"

Like prior perpetrators of schoolplace violence, Eric Harris and Dylan Klebold gave several indications of their violent intentions. Harris's Web site bragged, "Goodbye to all on April 20th . . . this will be my last day on Earth." Columbine's senior class picture depicts Harris and Klebold pointing their fingers at the camera in a fake gun gesture. Clothing, hobbies, class projects, and statements made by Harris and Klebold provided ample evidence that they were submerged in an obsession with violence in the months preceding the massacre. Despite these warnings and threats, attention given to these troubled youths was insufficient. And despite repeated evidence of such warnings and threats, on the parts not just of Harris and Klebold but of most perpetrators of schoolplace violence, the myth remains that these perpetrators are just "normal" kids who one day unravel and bring a gun to school.

Most people do not have a frame of reference for violence. Its unlikelihood, especially in a school setting, makes it seem like an impossibility. The students at Columbine High School were in shock over what transpired, and repeatedly echoed the now-familiar question, "How could it happen here?" When you don't have a frame of reference for violence, you tend to dismiss warning signs, or you talk yourself out of being concerned about them. This leads us to myth #2.

Myth #2: "He's Just Going Through a Phase."

Adolescents are known for experimenting with different images. It's part of their development. They try something on for a while, see how it works for them, and then they try something else. For those adolescents seeking negative attention, the more outrageous the image, the more intriguing it is. For the most part this exploration is harmless and short-lived.

Tragically, many of the practice behaviors engaged in by perpetrators of schoolplace violence so closely resembled this kind of run-of-the-mill acting-out that they were dismissed as mere attention-getting tactics. People who were in a position to intervene chose not to because they did not believe the perpetrator was a true threat. They believed he was just going through a phase. In hindsight, these potential protectors realize that with just a little uncovering, they would have found that the violent interests were not just a passing curiosity. In fact, violent themes had embedded themselves in almost every aspect of the perpetrators' lives. Even if this was a temporary acting-out period in the student's life, it was one that could have had, and in these cases did have, deadly consequences, and should have been investigated thoroughly.

Practice Sessions: Heeding the Warning Signs

When violence is premeditated, the perpetrator will often engage in low-level forms of violence to "test out the system" and his or her own courage. These practice efforts can happen either mentally through violent fantasies or physically against "lower level" targets. Without intervention, practice efforts can escalate from fantasy to violence against property to harassment to deadly force. When practicing behaviors are noticed, protectors must work to create barriers to further escalation.

When Michael Carneal opened fire on his classmates, he said it was to get people to notice him. "I don't know why I wasn't bluffing this time," he said, referring to other times when he'd shown his weapons at school. "I guess it was because they ignored me. I had guns, I brought them to school, I showed them to them, and they were still ignoring me." These firearm show-and-tell moments were Carneal's practice sessions.

We have already mentioned the skiing analogy. At the top of the violence slope the perpetrator begins slowly, but he soon picks up speed. Increasing the intensity and frequency of violence, the perpetrator accelerates down the mountain—until he or she reaches a tree. When a barrier is in the path, the perpetrator must make a decision: Do I slow down? Do I try a different trail? Do I turn a different way? The more barriers there are in the perpetrator's path, the more difficult it is for him to continue on his violent mission. The rest of the chapters in this section are about building barriers.

Perpetrators will often dispense information in very subtle ways. This behavior is known as leakage or seepage. Offhand comments may be made to friends, parents, or siblings, and are usually followed with a disclaimer ("I was only kidding"). Seepage can also come in the form of violent essays, songs, or speeches written by the student. "The FBI Report . . . asserts that leakage is 'one of the most important clues that may precede an adolescent's violent act'" (Columbine Review Commission, 2001, p. 94). All of these are variations on what we are calling practice sessions.

Threats

The first level of violence assessment involves analyzing threats. Of the students who perpetrated schoolplace violence, 75% are known to have made some type of threat before acting (U.S. Secret Service, 2000). All threats should be taken seriously, even if they sound ridiculous. Like threats of airline terrorism, violent threats in school need to be investigated, and at a minimum carefully documented. In the aftermath of the Springfield, Oregon, massacre, concerned individuals responded to numerous threats with swift action, averting further disaster. For example, a 14-year-old boy was charged with disorderly conduct and harassment after he was overheard discussing plans to return to school and shoot everyone. Witnesses reported seeing him make hand gestures simulating shooting people while on the school bus.

Making Versus *Posing* a Threat

The U.S. Secret Service (2000) makes a distinction between *making* a threat and *posing* a threat. Perpetrators are *making a threat* when they actually tell people about their intention to harm some person or some group. They are posing a threat if they are engaging in behaviors that indicate that they are intent on mounting an attack. Planning, preparing, and practicing all fall under the heading of *posing a threat*. Some people may make a threat and never really pose a threat. Others may pose a threat without ever making a direct threat.

Threat Assessment

Most threats are harmless—just students blowing off steam and not thinking before they speak. However, what has one learned about a person who makes a threat in a school context where no threats are allowed? Such a person may have impulse-control problems. He or she may be trying to manipulate or intimidate others. He or she may be defiant of rules, or may be making the threat as a cry for help or attention. In any event, all of these motives are potential indicators of future violence. If the individual continues to make threats after being warned to stop, one has learned much more. Investigators have a stronger case to suggest that an individual is intent on committing violence when the perpetrator has paid no attention to confrontations and consequences.

Threats should always be analyzed for credibility and seriousness, and the lethality of the student should be assessed. Threats can be nonverbal, verbal, or written, and fall into three categories: direct, conditional, and veiled.

Direct Threats

A *direct threat* is a statement of clear intent to harm someone. There is no ambiguity or doubt in the statement. Examples are "I'm going to kill you," or "I'm going to blow them away." A direct threat is punishable by law, and the authorities should be contacted in such an instance. An example of this type of threat, as seen in schoolplace violence, is "I'm going to kill every girl who ever broke up with me." Students who make detailed threats regarding specific targets are more likely to become violent than those who make vague threats. *Generally, the more specific the threat, the greater the concern overall*. If the student identifies the weapons to be used, the name of the target(s), or the time and place of the violence in the threat, immediate action should be taken.

Before the tragedy at Columbine, Eric Harris made numerous threats through his personal Web site. One direct threat that was reported to the police targeted a fellow student, Brooks Brown. Eric wrote, "God I cant wait till I can kill you people . . . especially a few people. Like Brooks Brown" (Gibbs & Roche, 1999).

Eric also made more general direct threats, such as "You all better f---ing hide in your houses because im comin for EVERYONE soon, and I WILL be armed to the f---ing teeth and I WILL shoot to kill!"

Conditional Threats

A *conditional threat* is a threat made contingent on a certain set of circumstances. Conditional threats generally contain or imply the words *if* ("*If* you don't give me what I want, you will pay") or *or* ("You'd better do this *or* you're dead"). This kind of threat is designed to manipulate or intimidate the target into compliance. The following are conditional threats. If these threats are not met with resistance and clear signs of intolerance, they are likely to increase, as they are often powerfully reinforced. Kip Kinkel made a conditional threat when he told a friend, "If I ever get really mad, I'd go and hit the cafeteria with my .22. I have lots more rounds for my .22 than my 9, and I will save one for myself" ("Kinkel's Friends," 1998).

Eric Harris also made several conditional threats, such as "If you got a problem with my thoughts, come tell me and ill kill you" and "I am the law, if you don't like it, you die." He made several conditional threats against the students who ruled the school. For example, he wrote, "YOU KNOW WHAT I HATE? When there is a group of a--h---- standing in the middle of a hallway or walkway, and they are just STANDING there talking and blocking my f---ing way!!!!! Get the f--- outa the way or ill bring a friggin sawed–off shotgun to your house and blow your snotty a-- head off!!" and "YOU KNOW WHAT I HATE!!!? A--H---- THAT CUT!!!!! Why the f--- cant you wait like every other human on earth does. . . . If that happens one more time I will have to start referring to the Anarchists cookbook (bomb section)" (Prendergast, 1999).

Veiled Threats

Veiled threats are the hardest type to address because they are often vague and subject to interpretation. These kinds of threats are very real for the recipients, but seem to lose some of their impact when repeated to others. This type of threat is easily minimized by the perpetrator, who can easily refute the receiver's account of the event. The perpetrator may say the recipient just blew the situation out of proportion, or that the threat was only intended as a joke. An agitated student who says, "I can see how something like the Jonesboro incident can happen. I'm surprised more kids don't go off the edge" is making a veiled threat. Before his shooting rampage in Oregon, Kip Kinkel referred to "doing something crazy tomorrow." This was also a veiled threat.

Veiled threats are often used as a form of harassment in stalking situations. These threats were a consistent theme in Richard Farley's letters to Laura Black before he hunted her down and killed four people at his workplace. He wrote, "You cost me a job, forty thousand dollars in equity taxes I can't pay, and a foreclosure. Yet I still like you. Why do you want to find out how far I'll go? . . . I absolutely will not be pushed around, and I'm beginning to get tired of being nice." Veiled threats are the most difficult to detect and to pursue because of their vagueness and their susceptibility to multiple interpretations. Overall context and the presence or absence of other disturbing signs are important when deciphering the significance of veiled threats.

When violence experts ask students about the perpetrator's threats made before the killings, students often say they "didn't know that they knew." In hindsight, these witnesses were able to say that the perpetrators often made comments or acted in ways that made them uncomfortable about possible violence, but that they had not known such comments or actions amounted to threats. Therefore, training for students is essential (see chapter 7) to help them learn how to identify threats and how to report them.

Responding to Threats

Threats that come to the attention of school personnel are definitely serious. Case studies indicate that school officials are usually the last people to know about a potential threat or even the prevalence of weapons in their school. The following newspaper excerpt illustrated the typical disconnect between students and administrators:

> Attorney General Heidi Heitkamp of South Dakota [said] that she asked children at a school assembly to stand up if they had ever

seen anyone in school with a gun. *"Every kid in school stood up.... Not one of them had ever reported (seeing) a gun in school."* (Lofholm, 1998) [emphasis added]

Sometimes threats have been heeded, but the intervention was insufficient and the motivation for carrying out the plan was strong. For example, when police found a loaded handgun in the locker of Kip Kinkel, he was immediately expelled from school. His parents had been able to get him into counseling and believed he was improving. Nevertheless, Kinkel carried out his plan.

The Center for the Study and Prevention of Violence (2001) recommends that schools widely publicize the penalties for making a threat. The CSPV recommends that those receiving threats not show fear. The person making the threat often assesses the victim's reaction by looking for signs of fear or shock. Threatening individuals feel powerful when they upset their victims. The CSPV also recommends that steps be taken to isolate the threatening individual and to call in additional security. Depending on the seriousness of the threat, schools may need to remove the perpetrator from the school and prevent reentry to school property while taking additional target hardening measures to protect the victim (see chapter 6).

Schools must have a standard policy and procedure for investigating all categories of threats (see chapter 4). Many institutions have adopted a modified *zero tolerance policy* regarding threats, and despite the controversy, we believe that this is the most prudent course of action (see chapter 6 for a discussion of the issues). Briefly, we define zero tolerance to mean that all threats will be subject to investigation followed by appropriate consequences, and that threats to kill or assault others will result in a police report, suspension/expulsion, or some similarly severe disciplinary action. If appropriate, immediate psychological evaluation and intervention should be provided in these cases.

Reporting threats to a central location or communication vortex is critical. The FBI (1998) suggests that schools set up an anonymous 24-hour "tip line" where students can share their information without fear of retaliation. Teachers should also be encouraged to report disturbing information to a person in authority. In many cases of schoolplace violence, perpetrators wrote papers or made videos related to their violent thoughts as part of class projects. At the very least, all threats should be documented and investigated, and the person alleged to have made the threat should be confronted. Additionally, it is of crucial importance that all threats be reported verbatim, because the exact wording offers insight into the perpetrator's state of mind and possible intentions.

False Bomb Threats

Some schools have experienced false threats made for the purpose of disrupting the school community. These threats close down the school, often at exam time, and are very frustrating for school officials. For example,

- In Allen, Texas, a school cancelled the last two weeks of classes after a dozen bomb threats were made in a single week (Zuckoff, 1999).

- Newport Middle High School in Newport, New Hampshire, was closed for many weeks because of bomb threats ("School Shooting Threats," 2001).

- On April 26, 1999—just days after the Columbine shooting—all but one of Washington, D.C.'s 17 high schools were evacuated because of bomb threats (Zuckoff, 1999).

The Bureau of Alcohol, Tobacco and Firearms suggests that there are only two logical explanations for a bomb threat. Either the caller has definite knowledge or the caller wants to create mayhem. If the caller has a strong suspicion that an explosive has been planted, he or she may want to minimize personal injury or property damage. In this case the caller may either be the person who placed the bomb or someone who has become aware of the situation. An individual might become suspicious of a classmate's reading material or of bomb–making equipment seen at the home. In this "real" scenario (the threat of the bomb is real), the caller will present supporting information that can only indicate that the caller is legitimate. He or she may have detailed specifics about how the bomb was made or where the bomb was located. In the "fake" scenario the person making the threat wants to create panic and disrupt normal activities. In this situation, the caller will not usually have verifiable information (Kennish, n.d.; MacDonald, Shaughnessy, & Golvin, 1977; Security Resource Net, n.d.).

Profiling: The Controversy

What Is a Psychological Profile?

A *psychological profile*, in this context, is a behavioral analysis of an individual who has a propensity for violence. The profile entails a thorough assessment of numerous aspects of the person's life. Traditionally, profiles have looked at personality traits, innate temperament, violent characteristics, habits, and exposure to violence (real or dramatized), all for the purposes of predicting future behavior. In the aftermath of the school shootings, profiles proliferated and checklists cataloging these traits abounded. Computer software programs were even developed as a tool schools could use to assess risk.

Since the causes of violence in adolescents are so varied, one standard "profile" of violent offenders is not very accurate or helpful. Profiles are not specific enough to allow identification of those students who pose a serious threat. The novice profiler runs the risk of underestimating or overestimating the violence potential of a student. Most of the checklists run a great risk of a high *false positive* rate. A high false positive rate means that a large proportion of people who fit the profile never become violent.

Mistakes such as a false positive identification can unfairly label and stigmatize students who stand out because of unusual dress or interests. Because student violence is almost always the result of several variables, it is strongly suggested that multiple sources of information be studied prior to drawing any conclusions. Later in the chapter we list variables associated with violence potential. It should be noted that this list is neither comprehensive nor exhaustive, and the actual determination of an individual's violence potential should be made by a professional who specializes in this area.

Note: There is no single variable capable of predicting violence. In the absence of disconfirming evidence, one can tentatively assume that profile characteristics are additive. That is, the more violence–associated traits or behaviors a person exhibits, the greater the probability that he or she may act violently.

What Is the Controversy?

Although there is a good deal of controversy surrounding the use of profiling, it is important to note the distinction between traditional methods of profiling and current profiling technology. At its inception, profiling was based on inductive techniques. That is, an overall characterization of a particular type of offender was constructed through various means, including broad generalizations, statistics, evidence compiled from similar cases, and the experience of the profiler. With this method, potential perpetrators were identified by what characteristics they possessed and how they matched the previously established set of offender characteristics.

Current profiling technology no longer attempts to place individuals into preestablished molds or to single people out based on certain characteristics. Current profiling technology is data-driven and is used on a case-by-case basis, with reliance on deductive methods. Physical and behavioral evidence—in particular, behavioral histories with an emphasis on violence indicators—are gathered and synthesized as part of an effort to suggest possible future behavior and thus assess the risk of future violence.

Investigators concentrating on preestablished characterizations, as in the inductive form of profiling, may actually overlook potential perpetrators. For example, if we use age as a criterion for assessing school shooters, we miss several atypical cases. Historically, offenders have fallen into the 13-to-18-year age group, and under the old profiling system younger children would have been ruled out as possible perpetrators of schoolplace violence. Nevertheless, there have been several instances of aggression among younger children whose behavior appears to be similar in style and motive to that of the perpetrators of schoolplace violence described in this book.

- In Memphis, Tennessee, on May 22, 1998, a 10-year-old student allegedly brought a loaded .25-caliber semiautomatic pistol to school, pointed the gun at a classmate's head, and said "pow." The student had apparently stolen the gun from under the front seat of his father's truck and smuggled it into school in his backpack.

- Less than 2 weeks earlier, also in Memphis, a 5-year-old student sought revenge on a kindergarten teacher who had given him a time-out. He brought a loaded .25-caliber pistol to school after taking the gun from his grandfather's bedroom dresser. The child presented a bullet to a fellow student and told him that he wanted to shoot the teacher and another student.

- In March 1998, an 8-year-old Indianapolis student sought revenge on a female student who had teased him about his ears. He brought a loaded .25-caliber pistol to school and pointed the gun at a classmate. The 8-year-old student had taken the gun from his teenage brother.

Revenge is a common theme in schoolplace violence. Access to weaponry is essential. If these incidents are copycat instances, and they may be, certainly younger children are experts at that. And these younger children do not always stop at showing bullets to their classmates. Andrew Golden, one of the shooters at Westside Middle School in Jonesboro, Arkansas, was only 11 years old.

Race, ethnicity, and gender are other variables often misapplied in inductive profiling strategies. More than one person has questioned why the school shootings have not been described as a race issue, because such a high percentage have been committed by white adolescents. Again, when determination of risk is based on these characteristics and not on behavior, potentially violent perpetrators may be overlooked or innocent individuals may be singled out because of their race or innate temperament.

Common Violence Indicators

The following sections outline both specific risk factors for perpetrators of schoolplace violence and general indicators of violence. General indicators are factors that are often associated with violence potential of any kind, not school shootings in particular. While several of the general indicators for violence were not found in all, or sometimes even in any, of the schoolplace violence perpetrators, they should still be taken into consideration when evaluating risk. At this time, the number of schoolplace violence perpetrators is statistically small. Patterns established with only a minimal amount of data may not prove to be reliable over time. The general indicators of violence listed here have been empirically tested and shown to have a valid link with many forms of violence.

Risk factors are those personal characteristics or environmental conditions that predict the onset, continuity, or escalation of violence (U.S. Surgeon General, 2001b). Research tells us that violent behavior is not a biological certainty, but results largely from a person's learning history or from a combination of learning history and biological development. It is known that the more risk factors a child is exposed to, the greater the chance that child will become violent.

Indicators Specific to the School Shooters

According to the experts (CSPV, 2000; Fey, Nelson, & Roberts, 2000; U.S. Secret Service, 2000), there is no working profile of a school shooter. Instead, what is recommended is that investigations focus on behaviors and communications. Suggestive patterns of behavior and instances of practicing for violent behavior should be identified and addressed as soon as possible. We have already discussed, in Chapter 2, the TOADS (Time, Opportunity, Ability, Desire, Stimulus) formula for predicting violence. The following is a more detailed discussion of some known indicators to watch for.

Evidence of Planning

Schoolplace violence incidents are rarely impulsive. Perpetrators often develop their plans over weeks, or in the case of the Columbine High School shooting, years. Two years before his deadly attack on Columbine High School, Dylan Klebold allegedly wrote in his journal, "I'll go on my killing spree against anyone I want" (Dedman, 2000b). The U.S. Secret Service has determined that over half of the school shooters came up with an idea to attack at least 2 weeks in advance, and that more than half had developed a plan at least 2 days prior to the attack (U.S. Secret Service, 2000).

Involvement of Others

In the overwhelming majority of schoolplace violence incidents, the perpetrator told someone about the plans before the attack. In over half of the cases, more than one person was told, and in one case 24 people were told (U.S. Secret Service, 2000). Usually, the people who are told are friends or classmates. There were only two instances where an adult was notified (U.S. Secret Service, 2000).

Evan Ramsey told so many people that he had an audience of two dozen by the time he launched the attack in which he killed his principal and another student. The rumor spread that something big was going to happen.

While perpetrators usually act alone in the deadly attacks, about half of them were influenced or encouraged by others (U.S. Secret Service, 2000). It is often others who have suggested the idea or dared the student to take action. It is often others who have purchased the guns or bomb-making supplies or have shown the perpetrator how to load and fire the gun. Disturbingly, in close to half of the schoolplace violence incidents, shooters were either encouraged or influenced by their peers. One perpetrator was told by his peers that he not only needed to bring a gun to school, but needed to shoot other students and the principal so that his personal torment could end. He did.

History of Perceived Injustices

Many of the schoolplace violence perpetrators have believed themselves to be victims of an unjust world. A few of them sought revenge on principals or teachers who had disciplined them. Many more felt bullied, attacked, or harassed by other students at school. This persecution often occurred over a long period of time and reached levels the perpetrators described as torturous. The U.S. Secret Service (2000) believes that these experiences play a primary role in motivating the students to attack. Barry Loukaitis, 14, who killed two students and a teacher in Moses Lake, Washington, had claimed that "someday people are going to regret teasing me" (Dedman, 2000c).

Evidence of Depression, Despair, and Suicidal Thoughts

Several of the perpetrators of schoolplace violence committed suicide. Many expressed thoughts of killing themselves—an astonishing 75% of the perpetrators either threatened to kill themselves, made suicidal gestures, or attempted or committed suicide. In fact, some experts believe that schoolplace violence may be a form of attempted *suicide-by-cop* (Trompetter, 1999a). *Suicide-by-cop* or *officer-assisted suicide* are terms used when an individual decides to end his or her life by provoking the police into using deadly force (Prial, 1999). While none of the schoolplace violence perpetrators have been killed by police, some of them have asked to be killed.

After he fired his gun at his classmates, Evan Ramsey put another shell in his gun and said, "This one's for me." He then put the barrel of the gun under his chin, but he could not bring himself to fire. When police arrived at the school, Evan ran through the hallway and then exchanged gunfire with the officers. He finally threw down his gun and surrendered.

Practicing

In almost every case, the schoolplace violence perpetrator did something that caused teachers, police, or classmates to become concerned. In over half the cases, this concern was shared by more than one person (U.S. Secret Service, 2000). In some cases, such as Littleton, Colorado, and Springfield, Oregon, there was significant police or school involvement prior to the attack. In other cases, the perpetrator made offhand comments that struck listeners as disturbing. For instance, one attacker talked about a plan to put rat poison in a cheese shaker at a local pizza restaurant (U.S. Secret Service, 2000).

Difficulty Coping With a Major Change

More than 75% of the schoolplace violence perpetrators had had difficulty dealing with a major change prior to the attack. In some instances this was a breakup of a relationship. In other cases it was a humiliating failure or a discipline sanction. Luke Woodham was reported to have said, "I actually had somebody I loved and somebody that loved me for the first time in my life, the only time in my life. And then she just, all of a sudden one day she broke up with me and I was devastated, I was going to kill myself" (Dedman, 2000c).

Previous Experience With Guns or Preoccupations With Violence

Extreme fascination with weapons, extensive gun collections, and shooting skills are essential indicators to consider when assessing the potential for violence. The student who continually discusses or carries weapons, names his weapons, or evidences an unusual enthusiasm for semiautomatic or automatic guns definitely presents a risk. This type of obsession may also apply to other weapons of destruction, such as explosives and bombs. Sixty percent of the schoolplace violence perpetrators showed interest in violent themes in video games or other forms of media or, more commonly, expressed interest through their writing (Dedman, 2000b).

Mitchell Johnson, 13, one of the team killers at Jonesboro, claimed to be a member of the Bloods gang. Johnson was from a small Arkansas town with no known gangs, yet he frequently wore red and would write the words "Crip killers" on notebooks. When he showed up to school on the day of the killing he was wearing head-to-toe camouflage fatigues.

Johnson's 11-year-old accomplice, Andrew Golden, was given a gun by Santa Claus when he was 6. His father had introduced him to "practical shooting," a competition where shooters attempt to hit pop-up or moving targets to simulate real-life scenarios.

The Secret Service found that over half the perpetrators had a history of gun use and nearly two thirds of the attackers got the guns from their own homes or the homes of relatives.

The students who evidence a preoccupation with violence will constantly talk about the subject and will find ways to expose themselves to further violence. Many enjoy violent musical lyrics (Klebold and Harris favored Rammstein, a group noted for such lyrics), movies (*Natural Born Killers* was a stated favorite with more than one perpetrator), and the violence-oriented sites on the Internet. Several of the schoolplace violence perpetrators evidenced this preoccupation with violent acts in their class assignments, their topics of conversation, and their extracurricular activities (many choosing violent shoot-'em-up video games). Kip Kinkel had told friends that he dreamed of going into the Army so he would know what it was like to kill somebody. Evidence of a severe preoccupation or fascination with violence is a serious risk factor for future violence. Youths' ability to generate alternative solutions to their problems is diminished as they increasingly focus on details of violence and fantasies of violent rampages.

Youths may carry weapons because they falsely believe this will make them safer (Pittel, 1998). Some students may carry a weapon to increase their feelings of self-worth in response to being bullied. In 1995, researchers Snyder and Sickmund found that 28% of inner-city high school students believe that it is "okay to shoot someone who hurts or insults you." Guns are not the only weapons to be on alert for: Other implements to consider in your assessment of dangerousness include edge weapons, explosive devices, and club weapons.

Non-Indicators for Potential Risk of Schoolplace Violence

There are a few indicators that have been looked into and have proven not to have a verifiable connection to schoolplace violence. According to the Secret Service report, for example, school performance does not inform us of an individual student's potential risk. Shooters' academic histories have ranged from top-of-the-class to failing. Nor do school discipline records offer a connection: Some shooters had no records at all while others had multiple discipline infractions. Strikingly, less that one third of the perpetrators of schoolplace violence had drug or alcohol problems. Only a few had been diagnosed with mental illness. The myth of the loner is equally unhelpful in identifying potential shooters. Some shooters were indeed isolated loner types, but others had many friends. Interestingly, few perpetrators showed any change in academic performance, friendships, or discipline at school in the days leading up to their attacks (U.S. Secret Service, 2000).

General Indicators of Violence

While the following indicators have not been shown to be specific to perpetrators of schoolplace violence, they are nonetheless predictive of violent potential and therefore well worth considering in efforts at violence prevention.

History of Violence

According to the adage, past behavior is the best indicator of future behavior. This is definitely true with respect to violent behavior. The probability of future violence increases with each violent act. Seriously violent children and adolescents often have histories that include the mutilation, torture, and killing of animals. It is known that young people repeatedly exposed to violence have a heightened risk of perpetrating violence (Knox, Carey, Kim, & Niedermeier, 2000). Some of the school-place violence perpetrators either were victims of family or peer violence, or had witnessed violence in their homes. Interestingly, very few of these perpetrators had a history of extreme violence against people. However, there was evidence of violence practicing. Mitchell Johnson had pulled a knife on another student. Kip Kinkel and Luke Woodham had allegedly tortured animals. Eric Harris and Dylan Klebold were known to cause destruction to property. Many lashed out verbally against others. A surprising finding is that these horrific killing rampages were usually the first instance of these students acting in a physically aggressive way against other people.

Unsuccessful Personal History

A student who has repeated failures within the academic setting may be at risk for developing low self-esteem. A person whose life is filled with failures, unattained goals, rejections, and unfulfilled dreams may choose antisocial avenues to reconcile the imbalance he or she feels in his or her life. The students involved in schoolplace violence varied greatly in their academic abilities. Gary "Scott" Pennington, Barry Loukaitais, Luke Woodham, Eric Harris, and Dylan Klebold were all above average or honor students. Mitchell Johnson and Drew Golden were average students, and Andrew Wurst was a poor student. Apparently, for the better students, academic success did not lead these perpetrators to feeling successful. In fact, being smart may have exacerbated their feelings of isolation. Loukaitis was taunted by peers for being a "nerd."

In many cases the schoolplace violence perpetrators struggled socially, either with peers or with girlfriends. In some instances peers had teased them by labeling them as homosexuals. This was the case for Eric

Harris and Dylan Klebold because they spent so much time together. Harris was known to be an outsider, but Klebold had several friends from different social circles. Both boys grappled with getting dates. Harris was turned down three times in his quest to get a prom date.

Substance Abuse

While substance abuse has not been directly associated with school shooters, it may still be considered a risk factor for violence. Interestingly, very few of the school shooters abused drugs or alcohol and, amazingly, almost all were substance-free when they committed violence. This pattern is very atypical for many forms of violence. Alcohol in particular has been associated with violent behavior because it lowers inhibitions to act. We know that alcohol decreases pain sensitivity, anxiety about future consequences, and tolerance of frustration. Flexible problem-solving ability decreases with intoxication. We also know that witnessing or engaging in prior alcohol-related violence plays a major role in the connection between alcohol and violence. Finally, alcohol abuse has a built-in denial mechanism: blacking out.

We also know that alcohol directly affects the brain. All parts of the brain are eventually impacted with excessive consumption of alcohol, but it is the frontal lobe that plays a critical role in judgment and behavioral inhibition. The frontal lobe is one of the first areas of the brain to be affected by alcohol, and thus, appears to lead to increased impulsivity and "acting out" behavior. The frontal lobe is also responsible for long-range planning, and when it becomes impaired, short-term objectives become more pronounced.

When we look at violence in the United States, 13% of adolescents who said they drank or used illicit drugs reported carrying a weapon at some time ("Drug-Using Adolescents," 2001). In contrast, only 4% of adolescents who did not report drug or alcohol use said they carried a weapon. Thus, just because our current list of common indicators does not include substance abuse, we should not ignore the question of substance abuse. Substance abuse and violence are statistically linked, and the statistics on schoolplace violence are still extremely thin.

Verbal and Behavioral Precipitants to Violence

To prevent violence, school personnel must be able to identify and classify verbal and behavioral patterns. Students can be abusive with words or physical/nonverbal conduct. If there is an incongruency between a student's verbal and nonverbal signals, the nonverbal communication is always more reflective of the person's emotional state. A student who says "I'm not angry" but is red in the face and clenching his fists is showing nonverbal signs of anger. As people grow older they find ways to control verbal behavior, but most are unable to control the physiological changes that accompany anger. Many times students who are confronted about their anger are unaware of the messages their bodies are sending.

All behavioral factors should be used to establish a student's violence risk potential. In addition, the absence of expected physical reactions to emotional situations can be an indication that the individual has serious emotional problems and may have little or no access to feelings. Individuals like this can commit heinous crimes because they lack empathy for others. They are without conscience. Several of the schoolplace violence perpetrators were described as eerily calm during their rampages. Harris and Klebold took this one step further and expressed outright pleasure while killing. This aspect of the massacre is one of the most disturbing for most witnesses and others affected by the killings because it is so discrepant from normal human response.

Verbal Abuse Levels*

Language often reflects the emotional or mental state of an individual and can warn of future behavior. Paying close attention to these signs in students—noticing what they say and how they say it—can help with preventive action. Verbal statements can be placed on a continuum from compliant to assaultive. The chart on page 100 explains the five categories on the verbal abuse continuum:

---

*Note: This detailing of levels of verbal and physical compliance is provided for educational purposes only. A team of trained professionals should be employed to analyze the risk factors present in the student's behavior.

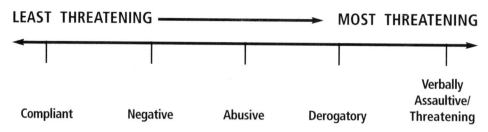

LEAST THREATENING ➜ **MOST THREATENING**

| Compliant | Negative | Abusive | Derogatory | Verbally Assaultive/ Threatening |

Compliant

The least threatening verbal declarations indicate cooperation and compliance. The student is not communicating any threat or resistance. This level reflects normal verbal interactions.

Negative

This level of verbal communication is basically pessimistic. The student frequently complains about a variety of things and responds negatively to helpful advice. This level of negativity is not necessarily dangerous, and some might argue it characterizes much of adolescence.

Abusive

As the student becomes more upset and distraught, the verbal expressions escalate to abusiveness. This stage involves general nastiness and name-calling. The student appears intense, blames others excessively, and frequently uses the word "you" in an accusatory tone. For example, "You never understand," or "You don't know."

Derogatory

The more the language deteriorates and becomes offensive, the greater the risk of violence. At this level, the student's conversation centers on making derogatory remarks, put-downs, and harsh criticism of others' ideas. Language is marked by vulgar, racist, sexist, and slanderous words ("You bitch"; "That fag"). The purpose of this language is to dehumanize the target. By turning people into objects, killers feel less connected to the consequences of their actions. This is a common defense mechanism during war, when soldiers turn the individuals of the enemy forces into something subhuman, usually through the use of racial slurs. Harris and Klebold were most likely not thinking of their victims as people with families and futures. They were killing "jocks" and all those with hats.

Verbally Assaultive/Threatening

This is the most serious verbal communication level. The individual is clearly threatening or attempting to intimidate others with language. Verbally assaultive behavior may include threats of physical injury and death. The more bizarre, destructive, and sadistic the language, the greater the risk of violence.

The lower levels of verbal abuse are designed to manipulate, intimidate, and otherwise control the behavior of others. Such talk suggests the student has minimal coping and/or interpersonal skills. While the lower levels of verbal abuse are not particularly dangerous, they do require attention and monitoring. The student who makes verbally abusive, derogatory, or assaultive statements is a serious threat to the population of the school. This student is likely experiencing an intense level of rage that could result in impulsive or destructive actions if timely intervention does not occur.

Physical Abuse Levels

Physical behaviors are also rated on a continuum from least to most threatening. Physically destructive or abusive conduct could reflect a deteriorated internal state or poor impulse control. Either of these can be a potential warning sign of violence.

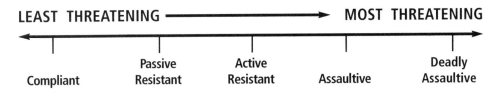

Compliant

A compliant person is fully cooperative and demonstrates the least threatening form of physical behavior. This level reflects normal youth behavior in its most desirable manifestation.

Passive Resistant

This type of behavior is also known as *passive aggressive* and is characterized by subtle defiance. Children and adolescents are masters of this type of behavior. They engage in resistive behaviors that are just under the threshold of noncompliance. They may follow directives but be extremely slow, putting forth only minimally acceptable effort. In a physical manner, they may use their body mass to impede another's effort by blocking a doorway, for example.

Active Resistant

This level of physical behavior involves a combination of actively resistant and passive–aggressive behavior. The student actively resists any form of problem resolution or arbitration, and may engage in subtle or overt defiance or alternate between these styles. There is a noticeable shift in the scope and degree of resistance. The actively resistant student is demonstrating signs of decreasing impulse control, and may show physical defiance toward authority figures. Examples of active resistance include slamming doors, turning over desks, or throwing objects. There is no actual bodily harm, but the threat of escalating violence is sensed.

Assaultive

The physical threat at this level is high. The student displays both verbally and physically aggressive behaviors, and is likely experiencing eroding impulse control resulting in a state of dangerousness. The student's intention is to harm or destroy either property or people. Attempts to gain compliance at this point are met with hostile resistance or attack. For example, the student may engage in an increased number of physical fights or attempt to hurt others with objects or vehicles.

Deadly Assaultive

The final category is the most extreme of physical behaviors and represents the greatest level of danger to others. At this stage, the student focuses on killing a specific target or a group of individuals, or on committing suicide. The potential for critical harm or death to others is high. Immediate remedial intervention, as detailed in chapter 9, must be instituted.

Chapter Six

Reporting and Timely Action

Zero Tolerance

"The message of zero tolerance is politically appealing, giving parents and communities the perception that schools are being tough on crime. While there are doubtless situations in which removing a child from school is necessary for that child or others' safety, at present we have no evidence that punishment and exclusion can in and of themselves solve problems of school violence, or teach alternatives to violence" (Safe & Responsive Schools Project, 2000b).

The concept of *zero tolerance* has come under fire lately, largely because of several well-publicized cases of egregious misapplication of the principle. The zero tolerance movement began in schools when the Gun–Free Schools Act of 1994 passed. This law mandated a 1–year expulsion for possession of a firearm on school property. Many schools then broadened the mandate to include other weapons, drugs, alcohol, fighting, threats, and even swearing. Then schools even began to take the concept to apply to behaviors that occurred outside of the school. At this time, at least one component of the zero tolerance approach is in place in over 80% of schools in the United States (Skiba, 2000).

Several problems arise from this approach. As Russell Skiba points out in *Zero Tolerance, Zero Evidence* (2000), traditional definitions of zero tolerance attempt to punish both major and minor incidents severely. Chronic offenders are treated the same way as first-time offenders. Basically, zero tolerance in this application is a one–size–fits–all approach. First graders are given the same punishments as twelfth graders, and students of color are often disproportionately impacted. This strategy is based on the assumption that sending a strong message about an unacceptable behavior will deter that behavior. Schools can "make an example" of someone in hopes that others will choose to avoid the same fate. Skiba details many cases that have made headlines because this approach seems senseless:

- A seventh grader, inspired by the movie *October Sky*, brought a homemade rocket made out of a potato chip canister to school. School officials suspended him after classifying the rocket as a weapon. The student was later invited as a special guest to the Space Adventurers' Annual Workshop in Washington, D.C.

- A 5-year-old boy brought a 5-inch plastic ax to school as part of a firefighter's costume and was suspended for bringing a weapon to school.

- A sophomore was given a 10-day suspension after passing nail clippers with an attached nail file to a friend.

Furthermore, traditional definitions of zero tolerance have relied heavily on the punishments of suspension and expulsion. According to Skiba, current research indicates that these are not effective deterrents to violence. The American Bar Association opposes one-size-fits-all forms of zero tolerance for this reason. Students who are suspended or expelled tend to fall further behind academically and risk engaging in criminal activity in the community (Martin, 2001). Studies cited in Skiba's report indicate that up to 40% of school suspensions are due to repeat offenders, suggesting that suspension is functioning as a reinforcer rather than a punisher.

Indeed, in some school shooting cases, the act of being suspended appears to be a catalyst, helping move the student from thinking about violence to acting it out. Thus, in some instances, suspending a student can actually increase the risk of violence at schools.

Zero Tolerance When Dealing With Violence

Perhaps paradoxically, in light of the foregoing, we are adamant that schools must be prepared to develop and enforce a zero tolerance stance against all threats and violence. What do we mean by zero tolerance? Do we mean that anyone who makes a joke about violence is automatically fired or expelled? No. What we mean is that every questionable statement or gesture goes under the microscope. Every threat gets addressed, even if addressing it only involves investigation and documentation.

The airline industry is currently the only trade that truly has zero tolerance for threats and violence. All threats or suspect behaviors are confronted—even jokes. In the aftermath of the postal-worker shootings of the mid-1980s to the early 1990s, many other workplaces have adopted zero tolerance programs involving tip lines and conflict resolution classes. The result? Homicides in the workplace have dropped by 20% since 1992 (Cottle, 1999).

A zero tolerance message can be clear and empowering, if properly expressed. Creating the policy may seem relatively easy, but enforcing it can be complex. Schools must think through what zero tolerance means for them. What is fair? What is legal? What fits with the mission of the school as a learning environment? Does it mean "one strike and you're out?" Many companies have learned the hard way that if you start shifting the line defining unacceptable behavior, the zero tolerance policy becomes worthless. When you enter situations where it's one person's word against another's, zero tolerance can become confusing. Effective zero tolerance policies take these issues into consideration, create effective means of enforcement, and train those affected by the policy to enhance civility.

Our modified version of zero tolerance can be used fairly and equitably. Russell Skiba (2000) labels this approach an "early response" model of school discipline. Using this model, schools can replace the one-size-fits-all idea of zero tolerance with a graduated system of discipline. Rather than set an example for potential violators with severe punishment for all, this system reserves harsh consequences for the most severe behaviors, while less serious behavior is met with less extreme responses.

The reason we retain the label "zero tolerance" is to underscore the importance of responding decisively. As we have seen in many instances, it is far too easy for people to write off threats and threatening behavior with rationalization ("It's just a phase," or "They're just kidding"). The zero tolerance label enforces the idea that all forms of threats will be taken seriously. For examples of alternatives to expulsion and suspension see the "Timely and Appropriate Action" section of this chapter.

The Communication Vortex

One of the lessons learned from the recent school shootings is that, though some persons did in fact notice peculiar behaviors or overhear disturbing remarks made by the perpetrators . . . no one person or group had access to all of this information. If there had been a way for students, teachers, parents, or others to report those isolated comments . . . then perhaps the whole picture would have been more readily discernible . . . (Center for the Study and Prevention of Violence, 1998b).

A communication center or communication vortex should be established to provide a knowledge base for all investigations. The National School Safety Center (1999) suggests that each district develop a mandatory incident-reporting system. A standard reporting form (page 108) and procedure will help ensure that reporting is complete and contains consistent information. This system organizes all incidents of violence by keeping records of the details of the incident, any responses, and outcomes. Any consultations, referrals, or other outside intervention should also be noted in these files. This documentation will help investigators determine patterns in perpetrators, targets, means, and other factors in their assessment of dangerousness.

In addition to providing documentation of critical or threatening incidents, the communication vortex can be a resource center for those concerned with violence prevention. The communication vortex can serve as a clearinghouse for the distribution of current literature and data on school safety issues. It can also house a list of local and national experts or others known to assist in finding solutions to school violence problems.

Reporting Procedures

Anonymous Tip Line

The International Association of Chiefs of Police (2001) recommends setting up a properly staffed, confidential hotline for use by students and staff wishing to report concerns about violence. If there is no funding for 24-hour staffing, answering machines or voice mailboxes must be checked frequently if the hotline is to be effective. The hotline number should be widely advertised throughout the school and repeatedly mentioned throughout the school year. Clarification should be made as to when to use the hotline instead of calling 9-1-1.

Internet Reporting

Another way to collect information regarding threats and potential schoolplace violence is through the Internet. Having students, parents, teachers, and the community make reports via the Internet through Web site submissions or e-mail is very attractive because it appears to be a confidential way to collect information about possible schoolplace violence all in one easy-to-access location. The problem with this medium of communication is that its confidentiality and security may only be an illusion. In reality it is fairly easy for a variety of people to hack into a school's computer system and access reports of school violence wherever they are archived. Once access is gained, a person would be able to see who made a report, when the report was made, about whom the report was made, and what the allegations were.

If schools choose to utilize the Internet in collecting information about possible schoolplace violence it will be important for them to educate potential reportees about the limited security and possible breeches of confidentiality that could occur over the Internet. Schools may also wish to spend the resources necessary to create a more secure computer system through the use of encrypted files and server firewalls. Schools could also enhance security by educating potential reporters on how to encrypt their own e-mails for added security.

Sample Report Form

The following sample report form was adapted from the International Association of Chiefs of Police's *Guide for Preventing and Responding to School Violence* (2001).

Threat Report Form

Date:_____ Name of threat-maker:_____ Year in school: _____

Person making report: _____

Title:_____ Phone number/e-mail: _____

Name(s) of victim or potential victim(s): _____

Relationship between threat-maker and victim(s): _____

What was the threat (actual verbatim account, if possible)? _____

_____

When and where was the threat made? _____

What happened immediately prior to the incident?_____

_____

Any other history that led up to this event? _____

_____

Describe any behavior that would substantiate intent to follow through on the threat: __

_____

_____

How did the threat-maker appear, physically and emotionally, when making the threat? __

_____

Names of others who were directly involved and any actions they took: _____

_____

How did the incident end? _____

_____

Names of any additional witnesses? _____

_____

What happened to the threat-maker after the incident? _____

_____

What happened to the other students or employees directly involved after the incident?__

_____

_____

List any consultations/referrals or other outside interventions: _____

_____

_____

What are the steps that have been taken to ensure that the threat will not be carried out?

_____

_____

Timely and Appropriate Action

Dealing With the Perpetrator

The type of corrective action needed depends on the nature of the incident and on past practice. The more serious the allegation, the greater the need for law enforcement intervention. Failure to act not only puts students in danger but can increase the liability of the school. Overly severe discipline, on the other hand, may infringe upon the rights of the accused student. As members of the Threat and Violence Assessment Team determine consequences, they should ask themselves, "Do the consequences fit the infraction?" Examples of interventions include the following:

- *Verbal or written warning and investigation.* In some instances, this type of consequence may be sufficient to address the seriousness of the behavior in question and to make an impression on the student body that all threats of violence are taken seriously.

- *Team meeting with student.* The Center for the Study and Prevention of Violence (2001) recommends that when a serious threat is made, schools should set up a mandatory meeting with the student and his or her guardians, a school psychologist, and a school administrator to review the circumstances of and consequences for the threat.

- *In-school disciplinary alternatives.* Attending school over the weekend or being confined to in-school suspension with a well-trained supervisor can keep the student both monitored and continuing academic progress.

- *Mandatory counseling, psychological evaluation, or skills-building classes.* With a highly skilled mental health professional, adequate rapport can be developed in mandatory counseling situations to explore the motives behind the threatening behavior. Psychological evaluations can help schools determine the level of risk a student poses while offering some educational opportunities for the student by getting him or her to become more self-aware. Skill-building classes such as those in anger management or conflict resolution can

help students build abilities for those social situations that currently are triggers for violence.

- *Restitution.* Students can be required to pay a fine or a fee for
mandated classes. They can also be required to participate in
clean-up or community service projects as part of their sanction.

- *Out-of-school suspension pending investigation.* In some cases where the
student is posing a serious threat, the removal from school may
be warranted. While this approach allows the school time to
conduct the investigation, research indicates that suspension is
not an effective deterrent to violence. If schools choose to take
this approach, they should be prepared to prevent the student
from returning to school grounds during the suspension.

- *Expulsion.* When no other alternative is appropriate due to the
extreme nature of the infraction, expulsion or the transfer of a
student to alternative educational settings may be required. The
International Association of Chiefs of Police recommends
suspension or expulsion for students who, on school grounds or
at school events, possess or use weapons that are capable of
inflicting grave bodily harm, or for students who physically
assault someone.

- *Legal action.* All students who pose a serious threat to the well-
being of another person should be reported to the police.

If the school plans to suspend or expel a potentially violent student,
it should be careful to escort the student from the premises, deny the
student access to the school, and take extra security precautions to
impede attempted reentry. During this critical time, there should be a
concerted effort to involve the parents and/or guardians in developing
plans to keep the student off school grounds.

Dealing With the Intended Victim(s)

When the perpetrator has targeted specific victims, school officials
have a duty to warn these individuals. People need to know when their
lives are in danger. Subsequently, all reasonable measures should be
taken to insulate the intended victims from the perpetrator. Often when

the perpetrator has been suspended or expelled from school some breathe a sigh of relief and let their guard down. More than one perpetrator has managed to return to school grounds after an expulsion to complete a planned act of shooting. The Center for the Study and Prevention of Violence (2001) recommends that schools set up a buddy system to bring together potential victims with other students or teachers to help prevent assaults on campus. We warn, however, that in some cases where the perpetrator is still a threat, this tactic may only increase the number of potential victims. Schoolplace violence perpetrators are not deterred by the presence of others. In fact, some of them want an audience for their violence and are not concerned about killing people who stand in their way.

Once the victims have been warned and the perpetrator has become less of a threat, officials need to continue to track the situation and make adjustments. Victims should be questioned about any needs they have or concerns for their safety. The International Association of Chiefs of Police (2001) recommends that the school provide the victim(s) with additional means to signal distress, such as cell phones or emergency transmitters. As with response to potential perpetrators, responses to victims should be along a continuum relative to the severity of threat and impact. Options for timely action for victims may include the following:

- Counseling and other victim services
- Additional security measures or communication devices as needed
- Safety training
- Consultation with law enforcement regarding various civil and legal options available to them
- Reassignment to a new school

Dealing With the School Community

The school community is also impacted by the threat of school violence, and timely and appropriate action is needed here as well. The Center for the Study and Prevention of Violence (CSPV) suggests that after a serious threat is made, a memo should be sent out immediately to all school administrators, school security staff, and teachers describing the threat and the school's response. Factual information about what is known about the situation should be continually dispersed to students and parents to update them on what is known and what is being done. This information must be sensitive to privacy concerns and judicial rights of the victims and perpetrator (CSPV, 2001).

Schools may consider increasing levels of security for a period of time in the aftermath of a major threat. These measures may protect schools against copycat behaviors as well as address immediate concerns for safety. In the aftermath of the tragedy at Columbine, many schools in Jefferson County, Colorado opted to have armed police officers guard school entrances. All those who entered Jefferson County school buildings in the summer of 1999 were required to sign in and state the nature of their visit. After a few months, security guards replaced the officers and the registration process ceased. The CSPV also recommends that when a student who has made a serious threat enters the school campus, special security checks should be required of that person.

Safety seminars open to the school community are also helpful. Self-defense classes and violence awareness classes can help the community feel empowered to address threats.

Chapter Seven

Training Strategies

A crucial component in deterring schoolplace violence relies on individuals seeing and reporting the warning signs of potential acts of violence. If this is to be possible, students, teachers, and staff need to be educated about the warning signs and possible indicators of impending violence. The training also needs to emphasize the importance of reporting suspicious behaviors to identified personnel.

Frontline Personnel: Teachers, Coaches, Counselors, and Support Staff

Those individuals who work with students on a regular and intimate basis are key players in the early identification and prevention of student violence. Too often, the warning signs of impending violence are missed, ignored, or misinterpreted by those individuals who have close daily contact with the perpetrators. An example of a missed sign, evidenced in several recent cases, is bizarre writing samples submitted by the perpetrators for class assignments. These writings revealed an intense preoccupation with death and/or destruction, and some included tales of animal torture or deviant belief systems (e.g., devil worship). Other examples of missed signs are veiled threats that are open to interpretation by the recipient. For example, Michael Carneal warned, "Something big is going to happen," but no one asked what he meant. Later his meaning became tragically obvious.

As former National Education Association president Bob Chase (1999) has noted, too often schools overlook the crucial role of support staff in their prevention efforts. Support staff constitute up to 40% of the public school workforce. Bus drivers, cafeteria workers, custodians, and others frequently feel powerless and uninformed when it comes to school violence. These individuals often see and hear things that would not normally come to the attention of teachers. Furthermore, because of job demands, these individuals are often at great risk for becoming victims of violence themselves. School bus drivers, for example, oversee dozens of children, and most of the time their backs are to their charges.

Training for frontline school personnel should minimally consist of an overview of what is known about schoolplace violence, which should cover

- Myths and realities of student violence

- A trend analysis: What has happened at other schools?

- Perpetrator characteristics

- Early warning signals and imminent danger signs evinced by students before they become violent

- Threats

- Barriers to reporting threats and disturbing behavior

- How to handle a potentially violent student

- How to handle a violent emergency

A significant portion of the training should emphasize early detection and intervention. The instruction should include the following:

- A description and explanation of the different categories of threats

- How to analyze the lethality and dangerousness of threats

- Steps that can prevent violence from occurring on school property

The training is best presented in conjunction with dissemination of the school's policy and procedure on violence. At the end of the training, the trainees should know to whom they should report suspicions and should have a general idea of what happens with reported information. A crucial aspect of the training is learning the specific steps to take at the different phases of violence: before violence occurs, when violence is imminent but has not yet occurred, and at the moment of violence (see Violence Flowcharts, pages 177–181). Schoolteachers should be instructed on procedures such as class containment during a crisis. The concept of "violence drills" should be introduced and implemented.

A violence drill is a simulation of an attack by a perpetrator outside or inside the building. This simulation can be conducted when children are in school or not. Schools run the risk of creating panic when running these drills unannounced when school is in session, but they will be able to best assess the effectiveness of their procedures under these conditions. Skills and procedures to be tested are described in chapter 9. These drills should be handled in a similar manner as fire drills.

Other training issues for frontline personnel include an understanding of the student culture and of reasons students might hesitate to report potential indicators of impending violence. The main point here is that if the teachers and other staff are hearing about it, the situation is already very serious and requires immediate attention and investigation.

Special Needs of School Resource Officers

School resource officers (SROs) are responsible for enforcing the law and protecting public safety. They can deter violence by being a visible, educating presence at school and by developing a rapport with students. They sometimes experience conflict as a liaison between the school community and the police department, and should be trained in how to make judgment calls regarding violence. Many are expected to function as friends to the students, consultants to the administrators, and public relations representatives—roles that can come in direct conflict with their duties as law enforcement officers. When conflicts do arise among these roles, SROs need clear guidelines on how to resolve them.

The Columbine Review Commission (2001) recommends that SROs be in uniform whenever they are present at a school. They should receive training similar to other first responders in case of a school crisis. Unless the information is privileged by law, school administers should provide SROs with all relevant information needed to assess risk.

Community Involvement and Training

Organizations such as the PTA, community education centers, and church groups can get training information out to parents and other community resource people who are in contact with students. The training for this group will be less comprehensive than that for the frontline group, as the student violence policy and procedures will not need to be covered. This type of presentation could be conducted in a 30- to 60-minute session covering the essentials of sign recognition, threat analysis, and intervention strategies.

School officials should seriously consider asking some community groups to join them in a partnership for school peace. Some potential allies include

- Parents and parent groups
- Business leaders
- All school building staff
- Student clubs and activity groups
- Area youth center staff
- Local community policing officers
- D.A.R.E. officers
- Social service agency representatives
- Juvenile probation and court staff
- Fire and rescue departments
- Civic club and association members
- School resource officers
- Youth church groups
- Clergy
- Local sports teams and other athletes
- Prominent local citizens

Once the alliance group is formed with all relevant participants, a needs assessment should be conducted to determine the vulnerable areas of the school, and accounts should be given of potential problems arising within the student body. A concerted effort to educate the public as to the importance of the issue should be undertaken, along with contemplation of intervention strategies.

Parents

Parents can be an invaluable resource for schools working to prevent violence. Their anxiety and concern about their children's safety can be channeled into solutions and involvement. Schools should offer parents suggestions as to how they can become part of the solution. The International Association of Chiefs of Police recommends that parents be trained to assist teachers and administrators in monitoring student behavior (IACP, 2001).

The Surgeon General's office (2001a) wants parents to be aware that peer behavior is the greatest risk factor facing their children, and advises parents to know their children's friends and to encourage positive peer relationships. The office recommends the following publications for parents in search of ways to prevent violence:

- *Bright Futures for Families: What You Can Do to Prevent Violence*, a booklet outlining steps parents can take to protect their children from violence

- *Make Time to Listen*, a brochure offering tips to parents on how to communicate about violence.

Both publications can be ordered online at www.mentalhealth.org/youthviolence/orderform.htm.

The National PTA (1999) and the U.S. Secret Service (Dedman, 2000c) recommend various ways parents can get involved:

- **Talk to Your Children**—ask open-ended questions such as "What do you think about...?" to start a dialogue about violence at school. Pay particular attention to grievances and bullying topics.

- **Don't Be Afraid to Discipline**—limit-setting and appropriate parenting skills are critical for preventing violence.

- **Know the Warning Signs**—attend training on violence assessment to be better able to know when your son or daughter is heading into trouble. Know that violent behavior is the end result of a process—perpetrators don't just snap. Focus on what students are thinking and how they are behaving, rather than personality traits. Have an investigative mindset—talk to students, corroborate information, ask about weapon-seeking by students.

- **Don't Worry Alone**—if you are concerned about your child's behavior, do not hesitate to get a professional opinion. If you have concerns about another child, report him or her to school authorities.

- **Gun Safety**—many of the school shooters brought guns from home, so it's important to periodically reevaluate gun storage if you keep guns at home.

- **Stay Involved in Your Child's School**—stay informed and get to know the teachers and administrators. Become aware of school violence policies and procedures. Join your PTA or a Violence Prevention Coalition. According to the National Crime Prevention Council (National PTA, 1999), when violence prevention is a community-wide effort, crime rates can drop as much as 30%.

- **Help Organize a Community Violence Prevention Forum**—help communities identify problems and create solutions.

- **Help Develop a School Violence Prevention and Response Plan**—give input into these crucial decisions and assist with the implementation of these plans.

- **Know How to Deal With the Media in a Crisis**—learn the basics of public relations (see chapter 8 for more information)

- **Influence Lawmakers**—write editorials for the paper, organize petitions, and send letters to your legislators.

Students

The best metal detector is the student. (Ronald Stephens, National School Safety Center, 2001)

It may be hard to believe, but many schools overlook those who are possibly most in need of violence-awareness training: the students. Students tend to know well in advance of school administrators when potential violence is developing, but they often do not know what to do with this information. Students need to receive violence prevention training from experts, and they need information about responding along all points of the violence continuum. This means that in addition to being given long-term prevention exercises designed to help them appreciate differences and build self-esteem, students need to be taught about what violence looks and sounds like, how to stay safe, and how to report concerns.

Training students presents a different set of challenges. The emphasis here should be on two lessons:

1.) How to identify various verbal and nonverbal threats. Veiled threats in particular are difficult to identify and students are often left "not knowing that they know" about these indicators of violence.

2.) How to overcome what is often referred to as the "peer code of silence."

Peer Code of Silence

School officials should continue to work to change the 'code of silence' dimension of the prevailing culture, by emphasizing to students that loyalty to fellow students has its limits. . . . (Columbine Review Commission, 2001, p. 97).

Why are there so many stories in which students fail to report their peers, even when these peers have brought guns to school and displayed them, or have made veiled or even direct threats of violence? Experts blame the "peer code of silence." Students often follow this unwritten, unspoken code in which it is understood that parents, teachers, and adults in general are the enemy, not to be trusted with information or secrets. During the training sessions, emphasis should be placed on altering this code of silence where matters of life and death are concerned. Adults should understand that this pattern of conduct is going to be entrenched and resistant to outside forces. Efforts to completely dissolve it are going to be met with strict resistance. The wisest course of action is to attack the code of silence in terms of the damage it can cause.

Overcoming Obstacles

The following are common thoughts that have operated among students who failed to report what later proved to have been blatant signals that a student was contemplating violence. These obstacles should be addressed directly in the training.

Obstacle #1: "I don't want to get anybody in trouble."

Many students are uninformed about what happens after a report of suspected violence is made. They may view reporting another student as getting that person in trouble, instead of getting needed help. This problem is a direct result of lack of information, and can easily be remedied by educating students about schoolplace violence and teaching them that a student who is making threats or otherwise showing signs of impending violence needs help. The students need to know their instincts are accurate and their concern is based on something real. In terms they can understand, students should be educated about mental illness, obsession, alternatives to violence, and warning signs that another student is potentially violent.

Obstacle #2: "He might come after me!"

A part of the peer code of silence may center on fear of retribution from the offending student. Statistically, this fear is unfounded. Although revenge is a common motive for all perpetrators, not once has a student who filed a report against a perpetrator been a target of such revenge. In fact, in the Columbine case, Eric Harris had made threats against another student whose father had reported Eric to the police. During the rampage, the gunmen let this student go unharmed. Students should be advised that very often the potential perpetrator is, in a disguised way, really asking for help. Students should also be assured that their confidentiality will be protected as much as is practical. As suggested in chapter 6, a 24-hour tip line can help witnesses report the existence of weapons and threats. Protecting the anonymity of the reporter is left to the discretion of each school. In some instances, complete confidentiality may be impossible. Even when confidentiality is strict, individuals who have made reports of this kind are likely to feel they have taken a great risk and that they need extra protection. Any escalation of threats against the reporter after identifying a potentially violent perpetrator should be addressed immediately.

Obstacle #3: "So what if he's violent? He won't come after me."

People in general are very good at using denial to ward off fears and anxieties, and young people are no less proficient at this than anyone else. Students may think that they are such good friends with the potential perpetrator that they could never be hurt by him. The facts here are that in the schoolplace violence shootings we have seen in schools across the country, a friendship with the perpetrator does not guarantee safety. Typically, the shooter is prepared to die and has few, if any, loyalties left when he enters the school zone to commit the crime. During the shootings, perpetrators may not be aware of where, or at whom, they are shooting. The danger of being caught in the cross fire is significant for everyone, whether they've been friends with the perpetrator or not. Students should be taught that no one is immune to violence of this sort, and that even friends should be reported if their behavior shows signs of becoming violent.

Obstacle #4: "I'm overreacting. This kind of thing doesn't happen here."

Most people do not want to believe that violence can happen to them. People are worried that others will think they're paranoid if they voice their concerns. Denial and mistrusting one's instincts can play a major role in permitting violence to occur. Students should be taught to listen to their gut feelings, because their intuition about situations and people is often incredibly accurate. "This kind of thing" in fact has happened in several schools, and in many of those schools other students had been very aware of threats and other signs of impending violence, but had failed to act on the instincts that might have guided them in averting a tragedy.

Logistics: Setting Up Student Training Sessions

The best training location is a classroom, which is conducive to small-group discussion. It is also a familiar environment in which to discuss emotional and often anxiety-provoking material. Ideally, the topics of violence should be covered within an existing mandated curriculum such as a health course. The atmosphere should encourage students to speak freely. The discussion should elicit from the students their experiences, fears, and attitudes toward reporting the danger signs.

The students should be provided with handouts (see p. 123 for an example) detailing topics to be covered, along with a signature page delineating the personal responsibility of each student in preventing schoolplace violence. Students should be asked to sign an oath attesting that they have read and understood what will be covered in the training, as well as the school's policy on threats and violence. Students should also promise to dutifully report any signs of suspect behavior. Students should be apprised of the extent of confidentiality that will be guaranteed them when they report their concerns.

It is not only high school and junior high school students who are in need of such training—younger children should also be taught about these things. The notion of talking to young children about violence may seem alarming, but, as we have seen, grade school and even preschool children have made serious threats and have brought loaded guns to school. Training for this younger group should cover basic concepts of violence and reporting procedures.

Handout for Student Training:
Weighing the Pros and Cons of Telling

What do you do when you hear a classmate threatening to become violent?
- You can choose to not act and ignore the threat, hoping there's nothing to it.
- You can choose to act by confronting the person, asking him or her about the plans.
- You can choose to act by telling someone in a position of authority.

Let's take a closer look at these options.

DOING NOTHING
This choice sets you up for the burden of knowing you could have stopped something potentially bad from happening. How would you be able to handle the guilt of knowing you had the information to stop the violence in your school?

CONFRONTING THE PERSON
This might set you up to be the target of the person's anger or violent response. How much influence do you feel you will have with this person? Ask yourself the following questions: Do I fear for my own safety? How do I protect myself? Can I get others in my group to help me confront him or her?

TELLING
If I tell my friends, I can get some feedback on what direction I should take.
If I tell a counselor I trust, I can pass the information to someone who will do the right thing.
If I pass the information to someone of higher authority, I will be sharing the burden of worrying with someone who can act, and I can still remain somewhat anonymous.

WHY SHOULD I TELL?
If your intent is to seek genuine help for someone, tell!
If your intent is simply to see someone get into trouble, you need to examine your intentions.

Telling sets you apart from playing the not-so-innocent bystander. The bystander is either paralyzed by his or her own fears, or believes that the situation is not his or her business or responsibility. When a bystander does this, he or she is giving a signal to perpetrators that what they are doing is okay. Perpetrators read the bystander's inaction as approval, and they gain momentum from this reaction. *Schoolplace violence is every student's business.*

Telling a trusted teacher, counselor, or other adult *is an act of courage and leadership;* it is not "ratting out a peer" or being a "narc." Students who threaten violence need help, which they cannot get if their problems are hidden. *Telling* your parents and asking for their advice *is an act of courage and leadership;* it is not an act of caving in to authority or disrespecting your friend.

REMEMBER: If your intention is to STOP, PREVENT, WARN, or INFORM, then TELL!

Chapter Eight

Public Relations and the Media

Public Relations Before Violence Has Occurred

The goal of developing effective public relations in schools is to be able to disseminate accurate and helpful information without causing undue worry. When schools are developing their comprehensive safety strategies, they will need to be able to communicate with parents and community members what they are doing and why. Done unskillfully, this could cause a great deal of uproar and backlash.

The National School Safety Center (1999) makes several recommendations for cultivating a supportive climate within the school community when dealing with violence prevention. First, schools should distribute a school safety brochure to parents, school staff, and students. This brochure and all other documents communicating what is being done to stop school violence should start on a positive note—"this is what we are doing right, here are statistics that indicate that we are still a safe place for kids to be," and so on. The brochure may also outline the important issues and solutions of school violence. A regular newsletter can update or augment the information on the brochure. Second, a school safety fact sheet can relay information about the school district's current statistics on crime, violence, and disciplinary actions. These rates can be compared to similar statistics within the local community to help in identifying any emerging trends. Finally, awareness campaigns and recognition awards can help create a positive climate for efforts at preventing violence in school. Logos, slogans, and promotional items can help spread the message even further.

Public Relations After the Fact

There are two ways to get your own one-hour TV special. One is to be famous. The other is infamy. (Gregg McCrary, retired FBI profiler, commenting on Harris and Klebold's interest in notoriety, cited in Simpson, 1999).

The Media as Potential Ally

The media can have a positive or negative impact on the community in the aftermath of a violent tragedy. On a positive note, during the crisis the media provide the quickest and most efficient way of informing the surrounding community and concerned others about what is happening. Parents who cannot reach their children have a means by which they can get information during the intense stages of a crisis. The media can also help inform the community about ways to keep safe and support emergency responders during a time of crisis, and can make people aware of resources for help.

After the crisis is over, the media can offer reports on how school communities can reduce the risks of school violence. They can broadcast public service announcements that support nonviolence. The media can encourage investigative reporting by advertising or sponsoring hotlines for reporting threats or other risks for potential school violence.

Unsurprisingly, incidents of schoolplace violence attract the full force of the press. Overnight, towns that have never been heard of before become household concerns. It is therefore important to have a pre-planned strategy for handling this phenomenon, and to know the rights survivors and school community members have with the media. In general, when working with the media it will be important to communicate the truth, control for and correct errors in communication, and prevent the media from becoming part of the crisis.

The International Association of Chiefs of Police (2001) recommends that law enforcement build a win–win partnership with the media through creative compromise. For instance, in Boston, television stations have voluntarily agreed to share footage captured by media during hostage situations. This solution minimizes the presence of competing media crews that might add to the confusion. These stations have also agreed to refrain from airing live coverage during hostage–type crises when such coverage would endanger police officers or hostages. In return, the police allow the media access to better locations for images and keep them better informed with frequent updates (Nicoletti, Spencer–Thomas, & Bollinger, 2001).

Appointing Spokespeople

As we mentioned in chapter 6, a communication vortex is a critical factor in controlling communication that goes out to the community, as well as in assessing and organizing information coming into the school. This communication vortex should be known as the keeper and sharer of information. Highly visible representatives should be located in the main traffic pattern on the school campus so that media personnel can find them easily. These appointed communication representatives must diligently verify all incoming and outgoing information. If the information cannot be verified, it should not be released. Speculation of any kind should be discouraged.

Once accurate information is established, it should be vigorously promoted both within and outside the school. School officials should not wait until inaccurate information has surfaced. Periodic information sheets, letters from the principal, or mass e–mails can help keep the school community up to date on developments. Key individuals who will be most likely sought after for quotes and perspectives on the situation should be coached and given written scripts to ensure that a consistent message is being sent from the school. To avoid a "no comment" response to a question that cannot be answered, provide the reason that the answer cannot be given at this time. Appropriate school officials should always return media calls, even when a call's tone may be hostile.

Well–trained spokespeople can be a tremendous asset to the school in these circumstances. Without an appointed spokesperson schools leave themselves open for the *village idiot* effect. Every village, or in this case every school, has an "idiot" who will be willing to give the press an inflammatory remark. If the media is bent on presenting a stereotype of the school, they will search for such an informant, and additional harm will be done to the school's reputation. Therefore, each school should identify one spokesperson and an alternate to handle the press in the aftermath of a crisis. All inquiries should be directed to this spokesperson to minimize confusion and contradictory statements. The crisis management team should establish guidelines ahead of time for sharing appropriate information.

The appointed spokesperson must be prepared to clarify questions before speaking into the microphone. To avoid potential distractions, the spokesperson should select a time and location based on comfort level, not on the convenience of the media. Cold-call interviews in the home, or during the normal business day, are unacceptable. When preparing for the interview, the interviewee should find out beforehand what questions will be asked and what direction the interviewer is planning to take.

Most reporters and other media personnel appreciate courtesy and professionalism, and will often reciprocate this treatment. That said, it is appropriate to put limits on what is allowable for media coverage. For privacy reasons, school administrators should deny the media access to classrooms. Potential interviewees can be advised as to limits they can impose on the media. For example, they can be given the permission by school officials to tell the media, "I don't want to talk to you. Please contact our spokesperson." During the interview, spokespeople should share information on what went right, show empathy for the victims, and reassure the community that everything is being done to resolve the problems.

When the Media Become an Impediment

The media can become part of the crisis through their physical presence during a critical incident. During the Columbine shooting, many photographers clamored to get as close to the school as possible to take pictures of the escaping students. In fact, the media arrived at Columbine High School with 50 satellite trucks and 750 journalists while the crisis was unfolding (Ferguson, 2001). This posed a serious safety risk, as the whereabouts of the perpetrators remained unknown at that time. Additionally, news helicopters hovering overhead added to the noise problem already present from all the triggered alarms and emergency vehicles (Columbine Review Commission, 2001).

Media presence was problematic not only at the scene of the crisis, but at other scenes as well. They were reported to be aggressive and intrusive at the hospitals when they tried to penetrate restricted areas to discover the identities of the victims. As part of the emergency planning process the Columbine Review Commission recommends that emergency responding agencies prepare themselves for how to cope with the wave of media attention that will probably hit before the crisis is resolved. The following outline of rights with the media may be helpful.

Table 8.1: Rights With the Media

The school community has the following rights with the media. While they may not all be granted, they should be requested to protect the school and victims.

- The right to grieve and recover in private.

- The right to say "no" to an interview.

- The right to request a specific reporter.

- The right to refuse an interview with a specific reporter even if the interviewee has granted interviews to other reporters.

- The right to avoid a press conference atmosphere and to speak to only one reporter at a time.

- The right to refrain from answering any questions with which the interviewee is uncomfortable or that the interviewee feels are inappropriate.

- The right to ask to review quotations in a story prior to publication.

- The right to demand a retraction when inaccurate information is reported.

- The right to ask that offensive photographs or visuals be omitted from airing or publication.

Adapted from Slover, C., & Tasci, D. (1999). *Trauma recovery handbook*. Denver, CO: Nicoletti-Flater Associates.

Part III

Responding to Schoolplace Violence

Chapter Nine

Surviving a Violent Incident

An important part of responding to violence is to give the school community permission to do what they need to do to keep safe without inflicting further harm. This may seem self-evident, but even when violence is imminent, ingrained habits may create psychological barriers to action. For instance, schoolchildren being trained in how to respond during a school shooting were worried that leaving the school building would get them in trouble. After all, they had always been taught that this is the rule. Generally speaking, we are rule-bound creatures. We may think twice in our evacuation efforts before going through an emergency-only door. We may hesitate before breaking a window while trying to escape. Students and employees must believe that if they act in good faith while trying to keep themselves and others safe, they will not be held accountable for breaking school rules.

Rules can be explicit or implicit. Implicit rules are the unspoken guidelines. In situations where violence is possible, schools must be willing to slay the sacred cows. They must be able to mete out consequences to perpetrators even if they are star players on the football team or children of school board members.

The permission to do what is needed to survive must come externally from school officials, as well as be developed internally. Students and employees must be able to give themselves permission to do what they need to do to survive.

Responding Instead of Reacting

The truth about surviving violence resides in a principle of physics: Action is always faster than reaction. The perpetrator of violence is always one step ahead of the potential victim because the victim cannot predict exactly what action the perpetrator will take. Only the perpetrator knows what will come next. That leaves the potential victim in a position of guessing or waiting for the action. When people decide to become violent, they have crossed the line of social acceptability and the "rules" of human behavior are usually discarded. Because prosocial norms no longer apply, predicting the perpetrator's actions is difficult.

Still, although violent individuals may have the upper hand through action, the potential victims are not necessarily helpless. When potential victims are equipped with survival strategies, they become strong contenders. *Responding* is much more effective than *reacting*. When people behave in a knee-jerk fashion when faced with violence, chances are they will make a decision that places them in greater danger. Under stress, most people's fine motor skills, perceptions, and thinking processes are compromised. Training in proper response can help people negotiate dangerous situations even when their performance skills are impaired.

Performance Under Stress: The Liabilities

Impaired Fine Motor Skills

When under extreme stress we tend to lose fine motor skills such as the ability to use our fingers for intricate tasks. Therefore, when building a response plan for violence, it is important to rely on gross motor movements like those made by the arms and legs, rather than on the fine motor movement of the fingers. When workplaces ask for a violence consultation for the purposes of evaluating their emergency response plan, a frequent criticism involves the many demands requiring fine motor skills. For example, many places of business have an alarm system for first-line responders. The alarm triggers are sometimes in hard-to-reach places and require a finger to press a button. Some alarm systems are activated by the punching in of a code. Even dialing the phone requires fine motor movement. All of these behaviors are compromised under extreme stress. Alarm triggers should rely on gross motor rather than fine motor movements, and emergency numbers should be preprogrammed for speed dialing.

Distorted Perceptions

When individuals are under extreme stress, their brains switch to a different mode of information processing called *cerebral acceleration*. The brain begins to sort through tremendous amounts of information quickly so that the best decisions can be made. The senses become acute. Most people who have experienced this phenomenon report that it feels as if the world has turned into a very surreal, slow-motion movie. Reality is altered. Perceptions become more distorted as people try to anticipate what will happen next. Very often objects in the environment seem to appear and disappear. An example of this stress-induced misperception occurs when a police officer makes an error in judgment. Under stress, officers make guns, knives, and other deadly objects "appear" (when the suspect is really holding something else) or "disappear" (when the officer, because of expectations in a given situation, is not suspecting danger). Officers have been known to draw their weapons on suspects carrying nothing more lethal than a soda can. In that moment, the shiny metal can is interpreted as a knife. Perception becomes reality.

Tunnel Thinking

When people are in traumatic situations, their thinking often gets locked into one mode. For instance, in workplace violence situations, employees often attempt to use the phone to call for help. They instinctively dial "9-1-1," as they have been taught their whole lives. Unfortunately, this strategy does not work in many places of business because the company phone systems require people to dial "9" first to get an outside line. Under tremendous stress, many people forget this procedure and repeatedly dial "9-1-1."

Given these shortcomings of human behavior under extreme stress, some schools may want to educate their students and staff about tactics to use when a violent incident is occurring. People cannot rely solely on instincts in order to survive a dangerous situation. As humans become more civilized and technologically advanced, they rely less on instinctual survival skills. In fact, many instinctive reactions are now inappropriate and possibly even destructive. For example, notice how crowds tend to behave when there is a fire in a movie theater. Typically, a mass of people will run hysterically toward the nearest exit, causing a big jam. For this reason people worry not only about being burned to death, but also about being trampled. Another instance of poor survival instincts in humans is running behavior. When a predator is chasing a prey in the wild, the prey will attempt to escape by running in zigzags, or with erratic movements. This makes them hard to catch. However, when humans are pursued, they tend to run in a straight line, thus giving an advantage to the pursuer, who can more easily predict the victim's direction of travel.

To survive a violent incident, people need to learn how to overcome inappropriate instincts, impaired senses and motor skills, and tunnel vision. Humans can learn much about survival tactics from looking at animal species. Running, scanning, camouflaging, and distracting are all skills that animals use to escape their predators. These skills can also be taught. For purposes of training, we have arranged the useful behaviors into four strategies: get out, barricade, hide, and play dead.

Survival Tactics

Get Out

If there is enough distance between the potential victim and the perpetrator, this is the safest course of action. If they are to get out of a violent environment, people must be able to scan effectively. At Columbine many individuals were saved when they found an opportunity to run from the scene. The images of students literally running for their lives have been etched into the memories of all who were glued to their television sets on that day. This strategy has been helpful in many other incidents of workplace and schoolplace violence, and should be the first rule for survival. For example, in the Ottawa, Ontario, Canada, bus terminal shooting of April 1999, many lives were saved when 300 building workers were quickly evacuated. Upon hearing the first shots, an employee pulled the fire alarm to alert people to get out.

Of course, when the perpetrators are outside, as in the case of Jonesboro and Stamps, Arkansas, the strategy changes. In these cases, staying inside actually increased chances of survival. The basic idea is that in order to survive, potential victims need to get as much distance as possible between themselves and the perpetrators.

Some brave individuals have intentionally stayed on the scene, choosing to wrestle guns away from perpetrators or stand in the way to protect other potential victims. All are heroes. Not all survived. The choice to put one's life in peril to save another is a personal decision that each potential victim faces. Getting out requires its own set of tactics.

Scanning

All senses are important when trying to locate a threat, but humans primarily use vision. When most people scan, they haphazardly make a quick check from left to right. This method leaves many areas unchecked and therefore potentially dangerous. When scanning the environment, it is important to look for shadows, movement, and any possible areas of concealment. It is helpful to consciously scan a 360-degree circle. By dividing the space up into "pie slices," an individual can methodically check the entire space from floor to ceiling, one "slice" at a time. In other words, you must "scan with a plan." Sounds can also indicate areas of danger. Potential victims need to cue into any sounds of movement or breathing.

Distracting

Distraction is a very effective tool because it creates an opportunity to escape. Doing something unpredictable throws the perpetrator off guard. Distractions must be processed, and this processing takes time out of a perpetrator's lethal schedule. The pause thus created may give a victim an opportunity to escape. Visual distractions are especially effective because humans are largely visually oriented. Eyes tend to follow the fastest-moving object. If, for example, a perpetrator is pursuing a potential victim and the victim throws an object to the side, the aggressor's eyes instinctively follow that object. Even if the perpetrator's concentration is broken for only a split second, such distracting action can create opportunity for escape.

Running

It is useful when fleeing to override the human tendency to run in a straight line and instead to borrow the snaking tactic from animals. Darting back and forth makes it very difficult for pursuers to anticipate your next move, and thus slows them down. Another human tendency that must be overridden is the tendency to glance over one's shoulder while escaping a pursuer. This behavior is problematic as it pulls off one's center of gravity, increases one's risk of falling, and slows one's speed.

Seeking Safe Cover

Once individuals are outside the immediate area of danger, they should *continue running* until they are in a protected area. Sometimes people get curious and want to stay in the periphery of the violent environment to see what will happen next. This choice could prove deadly. Better is the choice made by some Columbine students, who ran to adjacent neighborhood homes and knocked on doors until someone was able to let them in for cover. In planning for the possibility of violence, schools might want to identify other potential areas of protection such as churches, police stations, or stores.

Evacuation

Signals for evacuation commencement should be different from those for a fire alarm. If students hear a fire alarm, decoding errors might result. For instance, students may think they are hearing firecrackers when the sound is actually gunfire. Directions given to students at this time need to be direct, simple, and repetitive. Those in authority should refrain from using any "do not" directions, as often people only hear the command that follows. The command "do not exit the south side of the building" may be interpreted as a command to exit the south side of the building. The command "use only the north side exit doors" will be more readily understood. Authorities should point students in the opposite direction from where the violence is occurring. They should give students permission to use emergency exits or to break windows if necessary.

One of the most dramatic images from the Columbine tragedy is that of hundreds of students running from the building with their hands held over their heads. When law enforcement personnel are unsure how many perpetrators are attacking the school or where they are, this measure might be necessary to prevent the perpetrator from escaping the established perimeter.

All evacuation procedures should include a contingency plan. In the contingency plan consider what would happen if people evacuated the building, the perpetrator followed them out, and no law enforcement officials were present. We recommend that in such a case people disperse in different directions with the goal of putting as much distance between the shooting and the targets as possible.

Barricade

If it is impossible to get out of the environment, the next best option is to barricade. Survivors often put as many obstacles as possible between the perpetrator and themselves. Perpetrators who are on a spree killing will not want to interrupt their momentum to tear down a barricade. Therefore, potential victims must close and lock doors, close blinds, and turn off lights. The whole concept of "out of sight, out of mind" defines this tactic.

In many of the workplace shootings as well as at Columbine, potential victims were saved when they closed and locked doors to the rooms they were in, turned off the lights, and stayed quiet so as to not draw attention to themselves. This strategy is effective because individuals on a crime spree do not want any obstacles getting in their way. It is known, for example, that robbers will not spend any longer than 60 seconds trying to open a lock. If they cannot break it within that time, they will move on. Harris and Klebold operated within a similar time frame. They came across barricaded doors, spent a brief time attempting to get in while taunting the people inside, and then gave up. Perpetrators know they must operate at a high rate of speed because law enforcement officials are sure to arrive on the scene. Action that may slow perpetrators, like hiding and use of blockades, can therefore save lives.

Lockdown

Locking down a building is no simple matter; however, it is usually a very effective delaying mechanism. In planning for lockdown, schools need to be aware of several potential difficulties. For example, doors that can be locked only from the outside (e.g., from the hallway) leave the person locking the door in a vulnerable position. Keys for locks are usually kept in cabinets, and it may take significant amount of time to locate the right key for the lock. If locking doors is not possible, barricading doors can be equally effective. These are details that must be considered by violence prevention teams creating procedures for lockdown.

Hide

The chameleon is known as the master of camouflage in the wild. This animal blends in very well with the environment so that the predator will overlook it and not attack. The human predator is not an effective scanner and will most likely miss the person who is hiding above or below the line of sight. Within reasonable safety limits, people should try to find hiding places that are not in direct view of the perpetrator. When hiding, they must be as still and silent as possible. Individuals should check to make sure that nothing is sticking out where it could be seen. Clothing, hair, limbs, shoelaces, strange lumps, and shadows all may call attention to a hiding person.

Unlike many other perpetrators, Harris and Klebold searched for and found additional victims who were hiding under desks in the library. This appears to be a reflection of their determination and the calculated nature of their assault. Despite this apparent anomaly, the advice stands that hiding is a good way to increase one's chances of survival.

Play Dead

Many of the students at Columbine were trapped in lethal zones as Eric Harris and Dylan Klebold sought them out. There was no way to escape. Several of them "played dead" in order to fool the perpetrators into leaving them alone. This tactic, as a last resort, can be effective if the individual is able to remain utterly motionless. Controlled slow breathing and minimal startle response are difficult to achieve under extreme stress. The sound of the guns firing can cause people to startle and jerk. But the tactic has been successfully used. Most times perpetrators do not take the time to insure that individuals are dead. They are preoccupied with moving on to other targets or escaping pursuers. In a Greeley, Colorado, incident of workplace violence, Robert Scott Helfer raised his gun to shoot at a coworker while another woman lunged at him. Helfer's bullets hit the woman's hand, shoulder, and thigh, and she fell to the floor. Alive and in intense pain, she lay still until he left through the window. Playing dead most likely saved her life.

Guns and Knives

Weapons are easily accessible to high school students. A recent national survey conducted by the Josephson Institute of Ethics discovered that 1 in 5 high-school boys report having taken a weapon to school in the last year. Forty-seven percent of all students surveyed said they could get a gun easily if they wanted ("Survey Shows," 2001).

Even though many students apparently have knowledge of weapons, many are still unfamiliar with what they sound like and how they operate. Many survivors of schoolplace violence have mentioned that when they heard gunfire they immediately thought the sound was something else—firecrackers, cap guns, cars backfiring. Because of this decoding error, many choose to move toward the sound to see what was going on. Such a mistake can be deadly, as it was in the Andy Williams case at Santana High School. Here many students initially thought the popping sound they heard was fireworks and moved toward the noise until they saw people falling to the ground. Gunfire in real life does not sound like it does in the movies. To increase chances for survival, people need to be able to recognize the sound of gunfire and then think to move out of the line of fire.

Another mistake people make when responding to a violent individual is underestimating the lethality of edge weapons—knives, broken bottles, and other cutting devices. When people see a gun, they know that it has high potential for deadly consequences. Knives are usually considered less threatening, but they can also be used to lethal effect.

During training sessions, schools should work with local law enforcement to develop effective tactical strategies in dealing with knife-wielding assailants. Most people do not realize that a lethal striking distance with a knife is as little as 15 feet. An assailant could mortally wound someone by running at him or her from 15 feet away and the victim would not be able to respond in time to escape.

If we go back to the TOADS model of understanding violence discussed in chapter 2, we know that we must be able to control time and opportunity if we are going to be able to effectively intervene and stop violence. Most of the strategies we have discussed in this chapter are strategies for buying time. Lockdown and evacuation are the two final steps of responding to violence that increase the time it takes for the perpetrator to get to victims and decrease the opportunity for the perpetrator to have access to victims.

Chapter Ten

Emergency Preparedness

When Eric Harris and Dylan Klebold stormed Columbine High School, they were prepared with bombs to forestall rescue attempts by law enforcement. Their goal was mass destruction, and their plan provided them time to achieve this. Through much of their rampage they had complete control of the situation. Law enforcement did not intimidate them. In fact, the perpetrators intended to harm the police fatally in several ways. First they fired rounds out the windows at officers and booby-trapped the bodies of their victims with explosives. Because of these tactics and because Harris and Klebold kept in constant motion, law enforcement efforts demanded increasingly complex and cautious maneuvers. Police efforts were also hindered because police were unable to access blueprints of the school to help them in their counterattack. Harris and Klebold, on the other hand, had studied the floor plan in depth and had marked out critical areas for mass killing, concealment, and escape. The tragedy at Columbine was a premeditated siege.

Unfortunately, in our current times, schools need to prepare themselves for such an emergency state. Schools must develop not only policy and procedures to prevent violence from happening, but also plans covering the possibility of a violent emergency. Each school district should develop systematic procedures for dealing with different types of crises, including schoolplace violence. Law enforcement must be part of the emergency planning procedures. This point may seem obvious, but it is often overlooked (Columbine Review Commission, 2001).

The purpose of these plans is to instruct key people on how to handle an actual crisis situation in an effective and efficient manner. In developing plans, schools will wish to take the following factors into consideration. (Note: Have the Threat and Violence Assessment Team identify a responsible party for each portion of the emergency plan.)

Siege Management Kit

Essential in the case of violent emergency is a carefully assembled *siege management kit*. Such a kit should contain

- Blueprints of the school with exit routes clearly marked

- Important phone numbers

- Current school roster

- Information about main leads for water, gas, electricity, cable, and telephone

- Information about alarm and sprinkler systems

- Locations of hazardous materials and elevators

An efficient way to store and update much of this information is to do a digitally photographed walk-through of the school. Staff and student pictures can also be stored digitally for easy access. The kit should be duplicated and kept in several different places in the event that certain sections of the school are too dangerous to enter. This kit should be made accessible to law enforcement personnel as well. The efficacy of such a kit depends on its being updated on a regular basis.

The International Association of Chiefs of Police (2001) recommends that schools should consider using digital technology and computer databases to store photographs and demographic information for accurate and accessible identification during a crisis. In addition, the IACP suggests that schools create a system of *Knox boxes* outside the school building. Knox boxes are storage devices that allow emergency response personnel access to school keys at any time of the day or night.

Additional items for the siege management kit will assist with the evacuation and staging needs during a crisis (IACP, 2001):

- Name tags

- Pens, markers, and notebooks

- Hand radios and batteries

- First aid supplies

- Blankets

- Megaphone

- Caution tape

- Bus rosters and routes

Staging Areas

The staging areas for individuals who escape from the school should be predetermined, along with the locations for medical triage. A plan for reuniting surviving students and their families should be thought out ahead of time, and this information should be regularly dispersed to parents and students. In case of a schoolplace violence incident, this plan should be disseminated to the media to help those who are unaware of the plan or have forgotten it. Identify locations away from school where students and personnel might be moved and triaged. Establish a primary location and an alternate to serve as the emergency command center.

One important issue to consider with staging areas is that they should be set up farther from the school than fire staging areas, and that in some instances they may need to be disbanded quickly. Unlike a fire evacuation, where escapees are told to stay together until a safety signal is given, a violence evacuation may need to be fluid. Perpetrators can easily follow people out of the school building and continue shooting on school grounds. Under these circumstances, people should be advised to separate and run as far as they can from the shooter. Despite this commonsense advice, the training we receive for fire safety is so ingrained that many people believe they are safe once they have exited a school building—even if it's under violent siege. Instead of continuing to run once they exit school doors, some turn around to watch what will happen next.

On-Site Safety Equipment

Review available on-site safety equipment, its location, and possible uses. Be sure to examine exit strategies in case of a siege. Most exits were designed for escape from fire, not from violence. Examine building, grounds, and supporting areas for evacuation and concealment considerations.

Transportation and Communication Needs

Investigate crisis transportation issues—early closings, traffic flow, parking, and emergency vehicle access. Establish clear communication and command responsibilities, also designating alternates. Determine how to adjust the bell schedule to ensure safety during a crisis. Develop an emergency signal to alert staff that a violent emergency is occurring or might occur. This signal should be unique for this type of emergency. Develop another signal to alert staff that the emergency is over. Develop a communication plan that will inform students, staff, parents, and the community of the school's plans in case of a schoolplace violence incident. Develop a phone tree to enhance communication. This phone tree should mirror procedures already set in place for other forms of mass telecommunications. Some communities have the capacity to conduct a reverse 9-1-1 procedure where homes around a certain radius of the critical incident are alerted instantaneously.

Establish a procedure for creating a list of injured students and staff that includes their names and conditions. Establish procedures and networks for providing counseling and support resources. Appoint a media liaison (see chapter 8). Decide how the emergency plan will be communicated to appropriate personnel, perhaps through informational brochures, special briefings, training video, organizational newsletter, or staff meetings. Consider expediting communication by storing as much of the information as possible electronically, so as to have easy access to digital photos of the school layout and other visual aids.

The Internet may serve as the most effective disaster communication device available. Information can be updated as needed and accessed from anywhere. Web conferencing and broadcasts can reassure a shaken community. Chat areas can help survivors begin the debriefing process and have their questions answered quickly. The disaster management potential of this medium is just beginning to be realized.

Violence Drills

Evaluate the efficacy of the plan through regular violence drills. As with most planning processes, what looks good on paper may prove inadequate in a real situation. Identify conditions or situations that can influence the emergency response, then plan how these problems might be managed. Geographical location could cause problems, as could legal responsibilities. Schedule regular reviews as conditions and staff change. Particular attention should be paid to protecting students with physical or developmental disabilities.

Safety Reinforcement

Safety reinforcement measures are those strategies aimed at making it more difficult for perpetrators to commit acts of violence. These measures include use of metal detectors, video surveillance, armed security guards, and other security equipment. These strategies can often deter other forms of school violence including graffiti, theft, and gang activity, and therefore we do not discourage their use. But it must be admitted that *these measures are usually insufficient to stop school shootings.* Luke Woodham, when asked about a metal detector, said, "I wouldn't have cared. What's it going to do? I ran in there holding the gun out. I mean, people saw it. It wasn't like I was hiding it. I guess it could stop some things. But by the time somebody's already gotten into the school with a gun, it's usually gonna be just about too late" (Dedman, 2000c).

Chapter Eleven

Notification Procedures

Internal Notification

How Do You Notify Students and Personnel?

In the event of a large-scale emergency, schools should have an effective mechanism for communicating within the building. In the past, serious problems have arisen when there was not a formal system in place for notifying students and school personnel about the violence in progress. Notification, if it happened, happened entirely by chance, and usually panic ensued.

Schools must consider what will be the best communications approach in the event of an ongoing assault on the school. First, schools need to choose which method will be most effective—a PA system? Walkie-talkies? Voice mail? Whatever the method, there must be a back-up plan. And a backup to the backup. We call this *triple overage*. Chances are that a problem will emerge with one of the communication plans, so it is best to have three prioritized options and at least two people with knowledge of the operation of each communication method.

What Do You Say?

A common misconception shared by school administrators is the idea that a code is needed to communicate that an emergency is occurring. For example "Code Red" may mean that a violent act is unfolding. The problem with codes is that people forget them, substitute teachers do not know them, and if they are too subtle, many will not pay attention to them.

We recommend that schools, when communicating about an ongoing assault, be as honest as possible about what is happening, especially about the location of the assailant(s). Those making the announcement should immediately follow it with the direction to initiate the emergency protocol and move people to either evacuate the premises or go into lockdown mode, depending on the circumstances.

Issues for Frontline Negotiators

In most workplace and schoolplace violence episodes, the perpetrators were unwilling to negotiate. Negotiation tactics work best with those who are ambivalent about their actions. Most times schoolplace violence perpetrators are not. Furthermore, the primary motive in schoolplace violence is revenge, so there is not much a negotiator can offer these perpetrators. For some criminal offenders, violence is a means to an end. That is, violent acts such as kidnapping or robbery are the strategies used to get a different desired outcome, usually money. For the schoolplace violence offenders, however, violence is the means *and* the end. As we have seen, schoolplace violence perpetrators are often suicidal and feel they have nothing to lose.

Like other types of rampage killers, the school shooters do not try to get away. The *New York Times* database that analyzed rampage killings of the last 50 years found that while more than one third of regular homicides go unsolved—the killers are never found—100% of spree killers are convicted. Not one of the 102 spree killers documented got away. In fact, 89 of them never left the crime scene.

Perpetrators of schoolplace violence are not suddenly finding themselves in an unpredicted situation, as is the case, for example, with bank robbers who are besieged at the bank by law enforcement. These perpetrators are determined to carry out their missions and, in all incidents to date, have been resistant to options. Usually schoolplace violence incidents happen so quickly that negotiation is not attempted.

In fact, once the perpetrator has started killing, negotiation attempts can be deadly, and there can be no turning back. All interventions at this point should be tactical, with the immediate goal of stopping the assailant (see chapter 12).

That said, students and personnel may nonetheless find themselves in a position where negotiation seems like a constructive course of action. We recommend the following do's and don'ts for people in this frontline negotiator position.

Table 11.1: Do's and Don'ts for Frontline Negotiators	
DO's	**DON'Ts**
Do stay calm.	**Don't** provoke (e.g., scream "You don't have the guts!").
Do give them choices.	**Don't** be disrespectful (e.g., call perpetrators derogatory names).
Do keep them talking—time is your ally.	**Don't** threaten—remember they're the ones with the guns.
Do ask them what they need—generate options for resolving problems.	**Don't** give them ultimatums you can't back up.

External Notification

The school should develop a speedy and foolproof plan for notifying external resources such as law enforcement and rescuers. You may think the 9-1-1 system will be sufficient, but, as we have noted, the 9-1-1 system may be user-unfriendly in a crisis, as in situations where a panicked person is required to dial 9 before dialing the familiar 9-1-1.

Stickers on the phone can be used to remind people of the necessary 9 prefix. Or phones can be preprogrammed to speed dial 9-1-1. Another tip: Do not advise people to dial nine-eleven as shorthand for 9-1-1. People have been known to search fruitlessly for a number eleven on the dial.

Work with local law enforcement to develop a standard reporting procedure. Refer to the emergency preparedness chapter (chapter 10) for help. Remember that triple overage is necessary on external notification procedures as well.

Chapter Twelve

Neutralizing Schoolplace Violence

Levels of Intervention

To review: Intervention occurs at four levels. In the best possible scenario, first-level efforts are successful and the violence is averted. *Neutralizing* is the term we use to refer to what happens at the fourth level, the worst-case level, when the only option left is to try to stop, by whatever means necessary, an already violent assailant.

On the first level, schools must have detection and awareness procedures adequate to the situation. There must be systematic methods for keeping protectors aware of the signs and signals of potential violence. Anonymous tip lines and other streamlined reporting procedures can facilitate data gathering. Employee hiring practices, and to some extent school enrollment policies, must take into account background patterns of violence when assessing the risk of bringing an individual to school. Frontline responders must be aware of practice phenomena—and alert to signs that young people may be rehearsing for violence. Responders must be able to detect escalating threats and violent behavior and be ready to institute intervention efforts before something more serious occurs.

On the second level, if perpetrators begin to practice violent behaviors, schools must adequately meet these threats with obstacles that will slow down the perpetrator and insulate intended victims. At this stage, barriers and technology come into play. Protectors must be prepared with a range of barriers. Barrier efforts, as we saw in chapter

5, include questioning, confronting, and implementing consequences. The idea is to put a roadblock in the path of the violent individual. Technological barriers—anything from enforced use of ID cards to locked buildings to tear gas—are also designed to slow the perpetrator down and protect potential victims.

The third level of intervention involves strategic response. In chapter 8 we discussed how individuals must not only have the skills to escape or avoid violence but must also be able to give themselves permission to act appropriately when the situation demands. Schools must have well-coordinated response strategies both internally and with outside agencies.

When all prevention and intervention strategies have failed to stop the violence, schools must defer to law enforcement. At the fourth and final level, the goal is to use the necessary force needed to stop the assault.

Tactical Solutions

When violence is occurring and there are injuries and fatalities, the most important task is to stop the perpetrator as quickly as possible. The goal is to minimize injuries and death. *There is no point in negotiation.* From this point forward, the responses are tactical, with the goal of neutralizing the assailant. It is beyond the scope of this book and our expertise to offer in-depth suggestions about tactical proceedings for law enforcement; however, we feel that a few general observations are appropriate here.

The majority of schoolplace violence incidents unfolded very quickly. The U.S. Secret Service (2000) reports that half of the incidents were over in 20 minutes or less. This is not a generous time frame. In many cases the situation had ended before law enforcement arrived on scene. In these instances the perpetrator either stopped shooting on his own, was stopped by a teacher or classmate, or committed suicide.

Despite those rare instances when courageous adults or students step forward because they have a tactical advantage and overpower or negotiate with the perpetrator, such behavior cannot be practiced in advance, nor can it be reasonably recommended. The primary resource for tactical maneuvers must remain law enforcement personnel.

Communication

Intra-agency response is inevitable in a crisis as large as a school shooting; thus police and other emergency responders must be prepared for alternate methods of communication. From the earliest points of law enforcement's response to Columbine, communication problems developed because different agencies' radios used different bandwidths, which significantly hampered interaction between departments. The Columbine Review Commission (2001) noted that problems with the communication and command structure were critical in slowing the response during the Columbine crisis.

Rapid Deployment

The experts who testified before the Columbine Review Commission suggested that school shootings present a unique set of challenges for law enforcement because police do not, as they often do in other situations, have time on their side. In hostage situations, for instance, police are trained to surround the location, to call for SWAT, and attempt to negotiate with the perpetrators. SWAT teams are usually composed of officers who have other responsibilities and therefore may not be able to assemble and arrive immediately at the critical incident. At Columbine the SWAT response time was roughly 45 minutes (Columbine Review Commission, 2001). By the time they arrived, Harris and Klebold had already wreaked significant havoc on the school.

Experts from the National Tactical Officers Association are developing new approaches to training first responders in rapid deployment methods. This training strategy would prepare responding officers, not SWAT teams, for immediate entry into a school during a schoolplace violence emergency like that at Columbine. Various training programs are still in their developmental stages, but their goals are similar—to give first responders the ability to neutralize active perpetrators who are in control of a large building where a great number of potential victims are present.

At this time these programs remain largely controversial with law enforcement because of the great risk officers face. As things stand now the progress of SWAT teams is slowed because they methodically and thoroughly sweep areas for potential threats—whether they are hidden perpetrators or incendiary devices. These precautions would be largely sacrificed in a rapid deployment situation.

Rapid deployment is also very risky for first responders because the perpetrators have so many advantages. First, many perpetrators come to the school with firepower and bombs unmatched by law enforcement standard–issue weaponry. Second, perpetrators are highly familiar with the school layout and can easily maneuver throughout the building and into concealment. Finally, perpetrators may be able to camouflage themselves by blending in with the chaos created by their peers.

Rules of the new rapid deployment tactics include the suggestion that officers leave behind innocent and frightened people, some of whom may be injured, so as to pursue the perpetrators instead. Many officers find this notion hard to accept.

In the aftermath of Columbine, law enforcement response was also criticized by those who felt that the SWAT team's slow entry prevented critical medical care from getting to victims. The Columbine Review Commission report suggests, among other things, that one or more EMTs be included in SWAT teams so that emergency medical care can arrive sooner, or, alternatively, that one or more SWAT team members be trained to administer emergency medical procedures (2001).

Part IV

Schoolplace Violence Aftermath

Chapter Thirteen

Recovery From Tragedy

Ripple Effects

Your school's role is just as critical *after* a violent incident as it is in early interventions. In the post–incident phase, begin the healing process as quickly as possible. All members of the Threat and Violence Assessment Team should be involved in the recovery phase. An overwhelming number of people can be affected by such an incident, forming a ripple effect, as the diagram below illustrates.

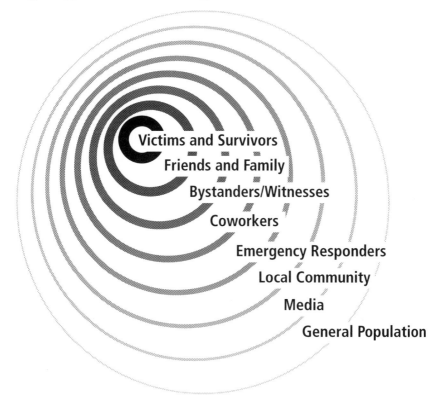

Victims and Survivors
Friends and Family
Bystanders/Witnesses
Coworkers
Emergency Responders
Local Community
Media
General Population

Critical Post-Incident Factors

After experiencing a violent incident or trauma, many people are immobilized by the shock and are uncertain what to do next. Prepared schools can help survivors know what to expect and what to do in the days and weeks following a critical incident. Analysis of schools that have successfully dealt with violence has revealed the following factors and themes in their approaches.

Leadership

Principals, teachers, key administrative personnel, and student leaders should be highly visible and should demonstrate intense personal involvement. In the aftermath of such a heinous crime, people not directly involved begin to make assumptions about the community in which the perpetrator resided. For example, the rash of school shootings in Arkansas and Kentucky led the media to speculate about the "southern culture of violence" as a contributing factor. Perceptions such as these are frequently unfounded and become detrimental to the survivors. In such a case a clarifying message should come from the leaders of the community: "This is what we are, and this is what we are not."

There are many instances that come to mind when considering the Columbine case. Principal Frank DeAngelis was open with his emotional reactions and repeatedly told the students that the way they handled themselves during this difficult time was inspirational. When he got to the podium at the April 25th memorial service, the crowd gave him a standing ovation, and he publicly wept. During the graduation of Columbine's class of 1999 he stated, "You are my special children, and I love each and every one of you." Columbine senior Amber Burgess spoke at the memorial service, and began the chant that unified the community: "We are Columbine! We are Columbine!"

Crisis Aftermath Task Force

In the aftermath of a tragedy, a predetermined task force can be instrumental in addressing the needs of affected individuals. The group can facilitate communication between the task force and those impacted, and can plan and organize the many post–incident events. *All affected groups should be represented on this team: teachers, administrators, students, parents, custodial staff, and any others directly involved.* This point cannot be emphasized enough. In the aftermath of the tragedy at Columbine, some felt that students were underrepresented in the "what do we do now?" discussions that ensued. Many were opposed to new security measures that invaded their privacy and worried that Columbine High School would become an environment hostile to students.

Debriefings and Victims Assistance

The purpose of debriefings is to offer a group discussion that incorporates education, information, and crisis intervention techniques with the goal of minimizing the psychological disturbance resulting from the traumatic event. The debriefings are usually offered in a timely manner and may need to be repeated over time. Participants come together to discuss their roles, experiences, thoughts, reactions, and symptoms of distress. Frequently, redescribing events in chronological order helps participants piece together a coherent account of what otherwise feels fragmented and surreal. Interventions should also focus on survivor strengths, coping skills, and social support. The scheduling of debriefings should take into consideration funerals and other memorials for those who died during the incident.

Professional mental health staff should be present to help facilitate the discussions and educate group members about normal stress reactions, symptom management, and when to seek additional help. It is valuable to remember that peers may be more likely than outside experts to understand the social circumstances and organizational factors particular to the participants. Help finding reading materials, referrals, and any other kinds of assistance and information should be provided as well.

In addition to debriefings, other forms of victims assistance are appropriate and should be offered as options. Mandatory counseling under these conditions is likely to be counterproductive. Schools should identify beforehand specific mental health resources that will be able to respond in such circumstances. One negative trend we have observed in post–violence situations involves the flocking of counselors to the scene of the crime. Some are well–meaning, others are sensation–seeking. Few are invited. At the reuniting area set up for students and parents after the Columbine shooting, counselors outnumbered victims and families. This is not uncommon. Following the crash of TWA Flight 800 in 1996, the American Red Cross announced they had gathered almost 500 volunteers, mostly mental health counselors, to help families. At the same time, another welfare agency was sending their grief counselors to the airport. Once again, counselors outnumbered victims.

Crisis also tends to attract people who are excited by the event and not always motivated by genuine concerns to help others. Many inexperienced counselors will abandon the situation when the novelty wears off or when they realize that they are in over their heads. The Emergency Support Network (n.d.) recommends the following steps to provide effective psychological assistance following traumatic events:

- *Decide beforehand who will provide psychological services.* Preplanning is important, as ad hoc responses can attract people who may be inappropriate to the task. The professionals you choose may be internal or external to the school organization. When deciding who should provide services, take into account the multilingual needs of students and their families.

- *Use an appropriate response time frame.* Haste is not desirable in this instance. Sounding the alarm for professional mental health workers immediately after the violent incident, setting up the expectation that this will facilitate a rapid recovery for the victims, ignores the practical needs of both the victims and the counselors. Such haste may even inhibit the normal crisis recovery process.

- *Offer practical assistance and referrals as appropriate first responses.* In the immediate aftermath of violence, victims may need mundane assistance. Transportation and financial assistance may be more helpful at such a time than counseling. Many Columbine students found that their cars were part of a crime scene for several days after the event. Transportation became a major issue in helping them reestablish order in their lives. Professional counseling is more likely to have a role after the immediate impact has passed, when victims are looking for something more than their friends and family can provide.

- *Provide a menu of services from which victims and their families can choose.* You might want to include on the menu a 24-hour crisis hotline/information line, psychological debriefings, educational seminars on how to help someone who has been through a trauma, post-trauma counseling, follow-up debriefings or telephone contact, and trauma-anniversary assistance.

Who Pays for These Services?

Victim assistance can be costly. In the aftermath of the tragedy at Columbine, several funds were set up for the multitude of donations that came in from agencies and private citizens across the country. Not all schools have been fortunate enough to receive such support from the rest of the country. The U.S. Department of Education offers a grant aimed at providing financial assistance to schools that experience a traumatic event. The grant can be used for security, counseling and support services, and translation services to help non-English-speaking families. The grant program is administered through the Education Department's Safe and Drug Free Schools Program and is called Project SERV (School Emergency Response to Violence). For more information contact the U.S. Department of Education at (202) 260-1862.

Ongoing Information Line

The International Association of Chiefs of Police (2001) suggests that schools set up an information line to help disseminate correct information to the school community in the aftermath of a large-scale crisis. This special call-in line can keep the community up to date on the status of any injured victims. The information given can also address any rumors and give correct information about what is going on.

Provide a Sense of Security

Increasing security efforts in the weeks and months post-incident will help reassure the school community that serious efforts are being implemented to prevent tragedy from recurring. In the immediate aftermath of a schoolplace violence incident, schools are at a high risk for copycat behavior. The FBI (1998) recommends that uniformed School Resource Officers be on hand to provide positive information quickly, and to sort through rumors about potential acts of violence. They further recommend that law enforcement officials have lunch in the schools on a regular basis in order to talk with the students and build trust. Post-trauma safety measures at Columbine included continuous sweeps of buildings for bombs and explosives, and a review of emergency protocol. During the first few weeks after Columbine, some school districts modified dress code policies to prohibit students from wearing trench coats like those worn by the gunmen.

Constructive Outlets

Often, people can find a sense of purpose and meaning in terrible events if they can channel their sorrow or anger into action. Additionally, tangible symbols of the tragedy can provide a sense of solidarity for the community. Following the tragedy at Columbine, for example, several factors facilitated the grieving process for those affected:

- Immediately after news of the tragedy broke, people began standing in line for hours at blood donation sites as hospitals announced their supplies were running low.

- Blue and silver ribbons began appearing everywhere—on jacket lapels, on backpacks, in storefronts, and in media images. It became the symbol of hope and recovery.

- Monument Hill at Clement Park, adjacent to Columbine High School, became a memorial site where hundreds of thousands of people from around the country came to pay their respects to the victims.

- Thousands of people attended a memorial service in downtown Denver on April 25, 1999. Songs written in memory of the victims, such as "A Friend of Mine" by fellow Columbine students, played on local and national radio. These musical responses to the tragedy carried a message of connection and support.

- Hundreds of banners and sympathy cards from schools and various organizations around the world were hung for public display at a nearby mall.

Donations and Memorials

Scholarships, survivor funds, memorial gardens, foundations, charity events—all have been successfully used to raise money for tragedy victims and give communities ways to pull together and participate in the healing process as a unified group. At Columbine, the outpouring of generosity from around the world was so great that the memorial funds became difficult to manage and caused a great deal of conflict. We recommend using an outside source to help manage funds in case such a situation arises. The United Way is one organization that provides such help. If the school has a Web site, you should consider creating a link for online donations.

Spontaneous memorials at or near the site of a death are commonly seen in America. For instance, roadside crosses at the site of driving fatalities remind others of the loss. Such memorials also emerge after school shootings. At Columbine the victims' cars were left in the parking lot when they became part of the crime scene. As the days passed, these cars were turned into shrines of remembrance. Such memorials serve a useful purpose, but they are temporary; eventually memorials of this type need to be taken down. This process must be handled with great sensitivity. Administrators must involve the mourners in the process, and may therefore want to consider making the dismantling of the makeshift memorial site a ceremony to mark a new phase of the healing process. Alternative permanent memorial markers can be installed on the site. A living memorial such as a garden or trees can offer hope and serve as a positive sign of renewal.

Follow-Up Services

Often immediate response to a crisis is excellent and thorough. As the fanfare dies down, however, attention may wander, and victims may feel abandoned. Periodic checking in with students, teachers, and staff will let survivors know they are supported in their continuing struggle to heal. Be prepared for significant dates for the survivors: graduation, birthdays, special dances, the restarting of school, and especially the anniversaries of the trauma (e.g., at 1 week, 1 month, 3 months, and annually).

Continuing Evaluation

After the intensity of the crisis has passed, all parties involved in the violence prevention, intervention, and aftermath should conduct a tactical debriefing as a group. The aim is to discover what worked and what didn't. The analysis and discussions of these committees should yield a report of lessons learned from the incident. Recommendations from the report should be implemented as soon as possible and shared with others.

Understanding Post-Trauma Responses

Not everyone who is victimized by a life-threatening situation is necessarily traumatized. Responses to emotionally intense experiences vary significantly, and are strongly influenced by personal history, coping abilities, available resources, and personality makeup. It is therefore unreasonable to expect that everyone who endures the same traumatic experience will exhibit the same—or any—symptoms and post-trauma reactions. In fact, suggesting there is something wrong with people who are not grossly affected may prove detrimental. People should be encouraged to "feel what they are feeling." It is important to remember that there is no standard way to respond to extraordinary events. Reactions will vary with individuals.

Volumes of books have been written on trauma and recovery, and we will not be able to address the complexities of these issues here. Please refer to the additional resources section at the back of the book for suggested further reading.

Trauma Symptoms

A schoolplace violence incident is a traumatic event and will likely cause strong physical and emotional reactions in many of those involved. These aftereffects are considered *normal reactions to very abnormal events*. During this time, the mind and body are trying to adapt and cope with a life-threatening situation, and will often spring into a red-alert survival mode. Victims may experience irrational fears, discomfort with previously enjoyed activities, and worries about family members and loved ones.

In addition to this activation of survival instinct, there is the impact of *shattered assumptions*. People hold assumptions about the world and about human nature. These fundamental beliefs are often not conscious, and they are quite resistant to challenge and change. According to trauma specialist Dr. Ronnie Janoff-Bulman (1992), these assumptions usually center on three themes: "The world is benevolent," "The world is meaningful," and "I am a good and worthy person." Most people believe that the world is a safe and fair place and that people are moral. From these core beliefs people derive their sense of trust, security, and invulnerability. The experience of violent trauma tends to destroy this sense of security, leaving victims feeling bereft and exposed.

Violence and trauma perpetrated by another human being is particularly harmful. Research summarized in Judith Herman's book *Trauma and Recovery* (1992) has consistently shown that trauma inflicted by another person is more damaging than that resulting from natural disasters such as hurricanes, tornadoes, and floods. Recovery from human-caused trauma tends to be prolonged and complicated. The disillusionment and *depressive realism* that can stem from such events can be paralyzing. The survivor becomes aware of the reality of surrounding danger and of the potential for loss. The implications of such awareness can become overwhelming.

In the process of trauma recovery, survivors learn to rebuild their assumptions by integrating the new traumatic experience. Talking with others, or writing about the event, can be very effective in helping to impose order on a chaotic event. By nature, humans are verbal creatures and need to put words to experiences. This is especially true for emotionally loaded incidents.

Another phenomenon associated with trauma is *survivor guilt*. When survivors blame themselves for what happened, it is often in an attempt to find some degree of control over an out-of-control situation. "If only I had done this . . . ," we hear victims say, or "If only I had not done that . . . ," or "Why did I survive when others didn't?" Such sentiments need to be dealt with. It is hard to be a survivor when others have perished. The random nature of the event is difficult to comprehend. Verbalizing their sentiments can help victims reestablish a sense of having control over their lives.

Finding some benefit or purpose in the experience can also assist with the *meaning-making process* for survivors. Many victims find it important to believe that the event happened for a reason. This drive for resolution can be aided by involvement in the community activities (donating blood, creating memorials, establishing recovery funds) previously discussed.

Post-Traumatic Stress Disorder (PTSD) is a psychological syndrome that affects individuals who have been exposed to a traumatic event and who are experiencing intense fear, hopelessness, or horror. To be officially classified PTSD the symptoms must last more than 1 month and must significantly interfere with important areas of functioning (e.g., ability to work). The cluster of symptoms, including nightmares, flashbacks, hyperarousal, dissociation, depression, and avoidance, was first noticed in WWI veterans returning from combat. It was initially labeled "shell shock," and then later "battle fatigue." Over the last several decades, research in the area of psychological trauma has discovered that other life–and–death situations—earthquakes, rape, domestic violence, airplane crashes, car accidents, and violent crime—can produce similar effects.

For many individuals, the symptoms gradually disappear with time, but for others, the symptoms can persist with varying intensity for decades. Many people erroneously expect that the "normal" course of a traumatic reaction spans 4 to 6 weeks. In fact, an individual cannot be diagnosed with PTSD until the symptoms have persisted for at least 4 weeks. According to the *Diagnostic and Statistical Manual of Mental Disorders*, 4th Ed. (American Psychiatric Association, 2000), the symptoms of PTSD fall into three categories: intrusive symptoms, avoidance symptoms, and hyperarousal symptoms. Each symptom can be understood as a coping mechanism as the body and mind react to the traumatic event.

Intrusive symptoms

These symptoms occur when images, sounds, smells, or tactile or taste sensations related to the traumatic event unexpectedly intrude into a person's consciousness. These vivid memories may be manifested during sleep in the form of nightmares. Others are triggered by internal or external cues that resemble some part of the trauma. When this happens, the trauma is repeatedly reexperienced. This can be quite distressing to the individual, and it is important to understand that this is all part of the normal healing process. With the survivors of the tragedy at Columbine, reexperiencing the trauma was a common symptom. Sounds similar to the fire alarms that rang through much of the ordeal have frequently been triggers for intense anxiety responses. Many survivors have had difficulty sleeping. Some hear the bullets and bombs go off as they try to sleep. Others wake up, "frozen," as one has reported, "seeing Dylan and Eric's faces."

Avoidance Symptoms

Reexperiencing the traumatic event is usually painful, so many individuals develop avoidance patterns to dampen the intensity of the uncomfortable feelings. For example, an individual with PTSD may avoid situations that are in any way reminiscent of the traumatic event. Others may become numb to emotions altogether. Depression and a loss of pleasure in life are common results of the withdrawal and emotional shutting down that can occur. The Columbine community has struggled with the issue of avoidance. Many believed that the library, where many died, should have been torn down and rebuilt. Some thought the same of the entire school. Other students said that they wanted to go back to school because, "If we don't, they win." Several students returned to Columbine more than a month after the massacre. One student retrieved her backpack, notebooks, and locker contents and proceeded to throw them in the trash when she got home, saying she "didn't want anything to do with it." The mother of the same student mentioned that her daughter avoids the streets that pass the high school.

Hyperarousal Symptoms

Individuals with PTSD often demonstrate hypervigilence, as they feel constant pressure to be on guard for danger. They may experience exaggerated startle responses, irrational and new fears, increased irritability, and explosive anger. They may have difficulty concentrating or remembering new information. Sleep disorders and disrupted appetite are common. The explanation for these symptoms is that some of the resources of the brain are being drained off to process the traumatic material. The troubled individual is operating at a diminished capacity—the usual reserves for emotional stability are significantly decreased.

Associated Symptoms

There are several associated symptoms that may be present when one develops PTSD. These include the following:

- Alcohol or drug abuse (the individual's attempt to self-medicate)

- Anxiety and panic attacks

- Suicidal thoughts, gestures, or attempts

- Extreme guilt

- Feelings of alienation or intense loneliness

If these or other symptoms persist for longer than 1 month, and interfere with the individual's life, professional counseling services with a therapist who is well versed in trauma should be sought.

Trauma Phases

Individuals who are traumatized proceed through different phases during the recovery process. While people may vary widely in their clinical presentation and array of symptoms, the general process among individuals is similar. Sometimes traumatized individuals will recycle through earlier stages when their traumatic experience is triggered. Others will proceed through the stages sequentially. There is not necessarily a right or wrong way to go through this process, and all time parameters mentioned here are general guidelines. Some people may move quickly through the phases while others may take years to come to resolution.

Shock

The first phase begins at the onset of the traumatic event, and can continue for up to a week. The perceived threat of death or injury is very real. Sensory information floods the brain. Sights, smells, sounds, and feelings overwhelm the individual's entire being. The brain is unable to process it all, and emotional numbness sets in. At the time of the traumatic event, there are often distortions in time and space, as well as auditory and visual misperceptions. The experience of events is in slow motion; there is an unreal or dreamlike quality to them. Sounds may be intensified, muted, or absent. Things may look different and unfamiliar, and there may be an intense focus on only one part of the visual field. There may be a strange sense of calm due to a survival mechanism of extreme denial in the presence of overwhelming danger. There may be some physical symptoms, including agitation, hyperalertness, over-activity, or biological disruption (e.g., sleeping and eating patterns).

Impact

This phase often begins when an individual leaves the location of the critical incident, and can persist from a few days to several weeks. This phase frequently triggers confusion and a sense of being overwhelmed as full realization of the extent of the danger, damage, death, or injury is made conscious. The individual may become highly emotional when leaving the scene of a disaster. He or she will likely feel a strong need to isolate, but should be with others for support and to ensure a recon-nection with people.

Recoil

This phase begins with return to a near-normal routine pattern, accompanied by stable days. There will be a decrease in the symptoms of the impact phase, while attention, concentration, reasoning ability, recall, and emotional expression gradually return. This phase often resembles an emotional roller coaster with good days and bad days interspersed. The important thing here is the stringing together of good days.

Post-Trauma Resolution

This phase occurs after a person returns to a routine pattern. Here the trauma's impact will show longer-term changes in behavior, thought patterns, beliefs, emotions, and perception. These changes may be irreversible. There are two possible outcomes of this phase: *positive resolution, or negative reaction with no resolution.* The positive course will lead to acceptance of the event and the individual's actions, along with a positive reevaluation of goals and values. Keep in mind, though, that this may be a lengthy process. The negative outcome is without trauma resolution. With the negative outcome there is a strong likelihood of chronic lifelong struggle with distress, family problems, job difficulties, chemical dependency, and potential suicide.

Some Basic Coping Strategies

Education

There are many excellent self–help books on the market today that describe the course and treatment of Post–Traumatic Stress Disorder (see the list of resources in the back of this book).

Healing in Stages

After a traumatic event, permanent losses and changes in views of the world and the self may mean that life does not return to the way it once was. Many assumptions about life have been destroyed, and developing a new set of beliefs will take time. Don't expect the traumatized individual to just "snap out of it."

Importance of Social Support

Victims, their families, and others affected by the violent event should talk about their experiences and feelings with others who are supportive. An organized psychological debriefing or support group could be arranged to help with this process. If there were others involved in the traumatic experience, it may help to establish regular contact with them when dealing with life after the event. Professional counseling should be considered if symptoms persist.

Empowerment

After the turmoil and intense emotional processing has passed, many people find they can derive strength from the knowledge gained from the trauma. Some people volunteer to help other trauma survivors. Others write about their experience. Some pursue legal avenues for compensation.

Epilogue

Looking Toward the Future

Schoolplace violence is a low frequency, high impact virus that continues to mutate. It is not a static form of violence, therefore future directions of this trend will be difficult to predict. There are many forces shaping schoolplace violence. Over the last couple of decades we have seen subtle shifts in the characteristics of the perpetrators, victims, and types of violent behavior. To stay one step ahead, or at least not too far behind, protectors must be willing to be adaptable in developing new prevention and intervention procedures.

The good news, though, is that through various trial-and-error approaches and current research findings, a compendium of best practices is coming into being. Schools and prevention agencies can minimize future losses with continued effort to share effective solutions. We can all hold on to the hope that someday there will not be a need for a book like this, as schoolplace violence becomes a thing of the past.

Appendix

Violence Flowcharts

The following appendix contains four flowcharts designed to assist school administrators in preventing schoolplace violence. Do not be caught unprepared. When a threat or potentially violent incident occurs, school personnel do not want to be faced with the question, "What do we do now?" Procedural and tactical intervention should be predetermined. The following four intervention plans are depicted in the form of flowcharts for easier conceptualization.

Plan A: Violence Potential Exists, but There Is No Immediate Danger (Page 178)

These situations develop when a student uses abusive language and/or gestures and makes veiled or conditional threats without a death threat. In these instances, it is important to investigate, document, and confront the alleged perpetrator.

Plan B: Immediate Threat Exists (Page 179)

An immediate threat exists when the situation involves direct or conditional threats ending with a death threat, and evidences aggressive behavior, including bringing a weapon to school. The goal at this time is to limit the perpetrator's access to the school. Notification to targets is crucial, as is a thorough assessment of the alleged perpetrator's dangerousness.

Plan C: Siege Situation (Page 180)

Violence is occurring. The primary goal is to implement the previously developed safety and evacuation plans in order to contain the violence and reduce casualties. Law enforcement should be immediately notified and may direct many of these steps.

Plan D: Aftermath Situation (Page 181)

Violence has just occurred. The primary goal at this stage is to prevent further violence and get assistance to the victims.

Plan A:
Violence Potential Exists, but There Is No Immediate Danger

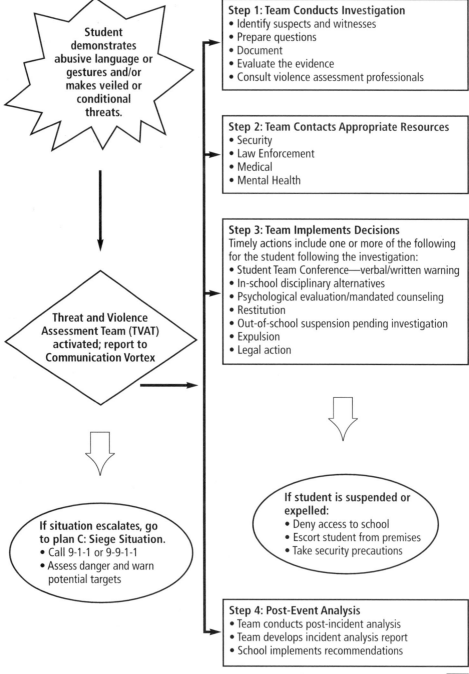

Student demonstrates abusive language or gestures and/or makes veiled or conditional threats.

Threat and Violence Assessment Team (TVAT) activated; report to Communication Vortex

Step 1: Team Conducts Investigation
- Identify suspects and witnesses
- Prepare questions
- Document
- Evaluate the evidence
- Consult violence assessment professionals

Step 2: Team Contacts Appropriate Resources
- Security
- Law Enforcement
- Medical
- Mental Health

Step 3: Team Implements Decisions
Timely actions include one or more of the following for the student following the investigation:
- Student Team Conference—verbal/written warning
- In-school disciplinary alternatives
- Psychological evaluation/mandated counseling
- Restitution
- Out-of-school suspension pending investigation
- Expulsion
- Legal action

If situation escalates, go to plan C: Siege Situation.
- Call 9-1-1 or 9-9-1-1
- Assess danger and warn potential targets

If student is suspended or expelled:
- Deny access to school
- Escort student from premises
- Take security precautions

Step 4: Post-Event Analysis
- Team conducts post-incident analysis
- Team develops incident analysis report
- School implements recommendations

Plan B:
Immediate Threat Exists

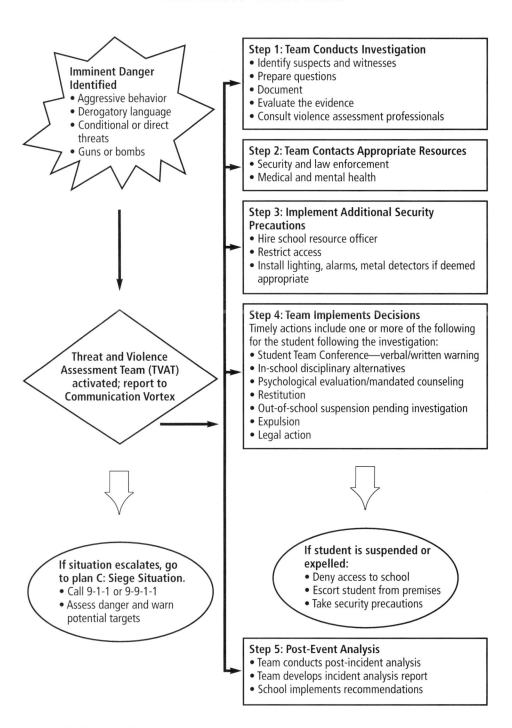

Imminent Danger Identified
- Aggressive behavior
- Derogatory language
- Conditional or direct threats
- Guns or bombs

Step 1: Team Conducts Investigation
- Identify suspects and witnesses
- Prepare questions
- Document
- Evaluate the evidence
- Consult violence assessment professionals

Step 2: Team Contacts Appropriate Resources
- Security and law enforcement
- Medical and mental health

Step 3: Implement Additional Security Precautions
- Hire school resource officer
- Restrict access
- Install lighting, alarms, metal detectors if deemed appropriate

Step 4: Team Implements Decisions
Timely actions include one or more of the following for the student following the investigation:
- Student Team Conference—verbal/written warning
- In-school disciplinary alternatives
- Psychological evaluation/mandated counseling
- Restitution
- Out-of-school suspension pending investigation
- Expulsion
- Legal action

Threat and Violence Assessment Team (TVAT) activated; report to Communication Vortex

If situation escalates, go to plan C: Siege Situation.
- Call 9-1-1 or 9-9-1-1
- Assess danger and warn potential targets

If student is suspended or expelled:
- Deny access to school
- Escort student from premises
- Take security precautions

Step 5: Post-Event Analysis
- Team conducts post-incident analysis
- Team develops incident analysis report
- School implements recommendations

Plan C:
Siege Situation

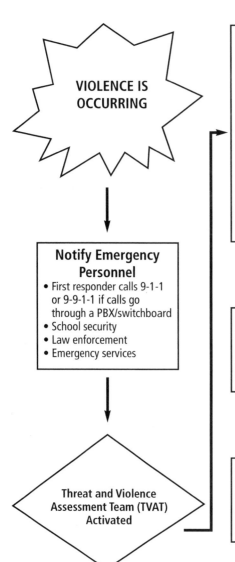

VIOLENCE IS OCCURRING

Notify Emergency Personnel
- First responder calls 9-1-1 or 9-9-1-1 if calls go through a PBX/switchboard
- School security
- Law enforcement
- Emergency services

Threat and Violence Assessment Team (TVAT) Activated

Team Leader Commands Staging
- Designate areas and personnel for the following tasks:
  - Triage the wounded
  - Identify location for students and families to reunite
  - Develop a central list for hostages, those missing, those who are safe, those who have been killed, and people who are injured and their location
  - Identify media headquarters and spokesperson
  - Notify victim assistance services
  - Notify next of kin
  - Address transportation concerns (buses, traffic flow, parking)

Coordinate With Law Enforcement
- Make facility blueprints available
- Coordinate additional phone services, food, water, and other supplies

Evacuate Premises and Secure Facilities

Continue With Plan D

Plan D:
Aftermath Situation

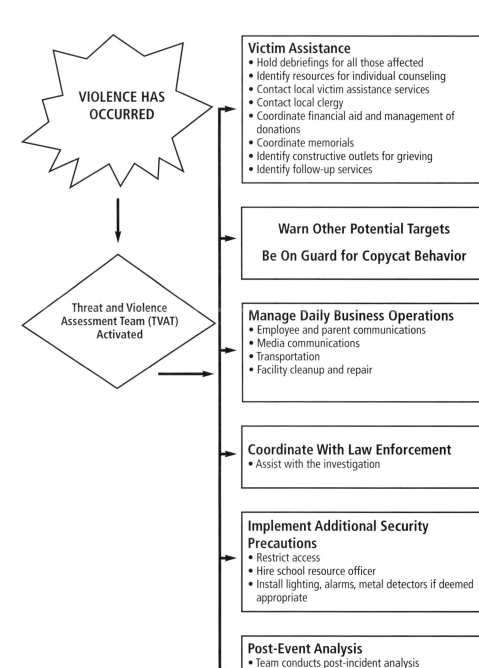

VIOLENCE HAS OCCURRED

Threat and Violence Assessment Team (TVAT) Activated

Victim Assistance
- Hold debriefings for all those affected
- Identify resources for individual counseling
- Contact local victim assistance services
- Contact local clergy
- Coordinate financial aid and management of donations
- Coordinate memorials
- Identify constructive outlets for grieving
- Identify follow-up services

Warn Other Potential Targets

Be On Guard for Copycat Behavior

Manage Daily Business Operations
- Employee and parent communications
- Media communications
- Transportation
- Facility cleanup and repair

Coordinate With Law Enforcement
- Assist with the investigation

Implement Additional Security Precautions
- Restrict access
- Hire school resource officer
- Install lighting, alarms, metal detectors if deemed appropriate

Post-Event Analysis
- Team conducts post-incident analysis
- Team develops incident analysis report
- School implements recommendations

Checklist for Interruption
of Schoolplace Violence

❏ Is there a Threat and Violence Assessment Team (TVAT) that represents the interests of all affected parties?

❏ Has a communication vortex been established?

❏ Does a zero tolerance policy for threats exist?

❏ Does a behavioral code of conduct exist for students and staff?

❏ Does a standard operating guide exist for investigations and consequences?

❏ Is there an effective reporting system for threats?

❏ Are all reported incidents reviewed, documented, and receiving appropriate action?

❏ Are violence professionals available for consultation?

❏ Have students, teachers, and support staff been trained in how to identify and respond to threats and practice behaviors?

❏ Are their adequate action plans in place to deal with identified threats?

❏ Has the Threat and Violence Assessment Team (TVAT) adequately addressed public-relations issues?

❏ Is there a trained media spokesperson and an alternate ready to be a media liaison?

Checklist for Responding to Schoolplace Violence

❏ Has the school developed a siege management kit?

❏ Does the emergency preparedness plan adequately address staging and evacuation concerns?

❏ Have school officials coordinated with local law enforcement to predetermine staging areas and safety procedures?

❏ Is there an effective notification procedure in place—both internal and external?

❏ Are there primary coordinators with at least two alternates on all of the critical responding tasks?

❏ Is there a standardized script for notification that will be comprehensible to regular and temporary staff?

❏ Are there effective lockdown and evacuation procedures?

❏ Has the school conducted violence drills with staff, students, and law enforcement? Have the notification, lockdown, and evacuation procedures been tested and practiced on a regular basis?

Glossary

Active resistant: A level of physical behavior that involves a combination of actively resistant and passive–aggressive behavior. The individual actively resists any form of problem resolution or arbitration, and may engage in subtle or overt defiance or alternate between these styles. There is a noticeable shift in the scope and degree of resistance. There is no actual bodily harm, but the threat of escalating violence is sensed.

Avoidance symptoms: Part of Post Traumatic Stress Disorder (PTSD). These symptoms occur because reexperiencing the traumatic event is usually painful. Many survivors of trauma develop avoidance patterns to dampen the intensity of the uncomfortable feelings. For example, an individual with PTSD may avoid situations that are in any way reminiscent of the traumatic event. Others may become numb to emotions altogether. Depression and a loss of pleasure in life are common results of the withdrawal and emotional shutting down that occur.

Barriers: Obstacles that slow down or stop a perpetrator's progress toward violence. Barrier efforts include questioning, confronting, and implementing consequences.

Bullying: A "form of aggressive behavior with an imbalance of power [in which] the dominant person(s) intentionally and repeatedly cause distress by tormenting or harassing another less dominant person(s)" (Atlas & Pepler, 1998, p. 86). Bullying can be direct (physical attacks, intimidation, name–calling), or it can be indirect (gossip, ostracism).

Cerebral acceleration: A reaction during a traumatic event where the brain begins to sort through tremendous amounts of information quickly so that the best decisions can be made. Senses become acute. Most people who have experienced this phenomenon report that it feels as if the world has turned into a very surreal, slow–motion movie.

Communication vortex: A reporting and clearinghouse system that organizes all incidents of violence by keeping records of the details of the incident, interventions, and outcomes. This documentation will help investigators determine patterns in perpetrators, targets, means, or other factors in their assessment of potential danger. The communication vortex can serve as a clearinghouse for the distribution of current literature and data on school safety issues. It can also house a list of local and national experts or others known to assist in finding solutions to school violence problems.

Conditional threat: A threat made contingent on a certain set of circumstances. Conditional threats generally contain or imply the words *if* ("*If* you don't give me what I want, you will pay") or *or* ("You'd better do this *or* you're dead"). This kind of threat is designed to manipulate or intimidate the target into compliance.

Copycat phenomenon: Term applied when similar acts of violence occur within close physical proximity or within a short time of each other and their similarities suggest that latter acts were conceived in response to prior acts. Copycat behaviors are common because children are extremely susceptible to the influences of social learning.

Critical period: The time during which a potential target is especially vulnerable to an act of violence. The critical period generally lasts from 24 hours to 2 or 3 weeks following the triggering event. Although it has not occurred in schoolplace violence yet, an issue that has affected workplace violence is an anticipated triggering event that extends the critical period for a period of days *before* an anticipated stimulus (e.g., commencement of jail sentence).

Defamation of character: Occurs when unprivileged communication containing a false statement intended to harm the reputation of another is released to a third person. Defamation of character is a possible liability issue for schools that are attempting to iden-tify students at risk for violence. To protect against the possibility of defamation, make the findings of an investigation and other pertinent documents available only to persons having a legitimate connection or interest in them.

Depressive realism: Occurs when a traumatic event has destroyed a person's sense of trust, security, and invulnerability. The survivor becomes aware of the reality of surrounding danger and of the potential for loss. The implications can become overwhelming.

Derogatory language: A warning sign of potential violence marked by offensive remarks, put-downs, and harsh criticism of others' ideas. Language contains vulgar, racist, sexist, and slanderous words intended to dehumanize the target.

Desensitization: A psychological and physiological process whereby individuals habituate to a stimulus with repeated exposure. People become desensitized to violence when they have been around it so much that it does not upset them anymore.

Direct threat: A direct statement expressing intent to harm someone or something. The more specific the threat is, the greater the cause for concern. Direct threats may identify target(s) and a means, and should be recorded verbatim.

Fads: Cyclical enthusiasms, commonplace in American culture. Fads gain much attention in a short period and fade out just as quickly. With violence, fads are often created through urban myths—stories that are well-known but have no basis in reality.

False positive: A problem seen in violence assessment when people use inductive means of profiling. In these situations a large proportion of people who fit the profile never become violent. They have been falsely identified as being at risk or potentially violent.

Fourth degree of victimization: Occurs at the community level. Many victims of school shootings and their families are often deeply integrated in the surrounding community. The victims and their families are church members, employees, neighbors, volunteers, and patrons of local businesses. These community establishments also experience shock and grief. Wider still is the world community, watching the tragic events unfold on their television screens and experiencing the horror of the fact that it has happened yet again.

Hyperarousal symptoms: Part of Post Traumatic Stress Disorder (PTSD). These symptoms occur when individuals demonstrate hypervigilence—a feeling of constant pressure to be on guard for danger. They may experience exaggerated startle responses, irrational and new fears, increased irritability, and explosive anger. They may have difficulty concentrating or remembering new information. Sleep disorders and disrupted appetite are common.

Intrusive symptoms: Part of Post Traumatic Stress Disorder (PTSD). Victims of trauma find that images, sounds, smells, or tactile or taste sensations related to the traumatic event unexpectedly intrude into their consciousness. These vivid memories may be manifested during sleep in the form of nightmares. Others are triggered by internal or external cues that resemble some part of the trauma. When this happens, the trauma is repeatedly reexperienced.

Killing teams: Schoolplace violence perpetrators who do not act alone in the actual shooting. Two individuals working together are especially dangerous, as they may experience a social reinforcement aspect and a pressure not to let each other down. They also reinforce each other's perception of perceived injustices, creating a sense of "us" versus "them." When there are more perpetrators, there will be more victims.

Leakage: A type of practice session schoolplace violence perpetrators engage in where they release bits of information regarding their plan to friends, family, and classmates prior to the attack.

Making a threat: Directly stating that you intend to harm someone or something (may be direct or conditional).

Meaning–making process: Sometimes occurs after a traumatic event when survivors attempt to find some benefit or purpose in the experience. This drive for resolution can be aided by participation in community activities.

Near misses: Plans for schoolplace violence that were foiled because someone discovered the plan, someone reported it to appropriate authorities, or someone interrupted the violence effectively.

Passive resistant: Behavior also known as **passive aggressive** that is characterized by subtle defiance. Children and adolescents are masters of this type of behavior. They engage in resistive behaviors that are just under the threshold of noncompliance. They may follow directives but be extremely slow, putting forth only minimally acceptable effort.

Pathway to violence: A series of events that when experienced by certain individuals can result in violence. The series involves (1) perceived injustice, (2) attempted resolution, (3) violent fantasies and practice attempts, and (4) confusion between fantasy and reality.

Perceived injustice: The first stage in the pathway to violence. An event or series of events occur and result in some form of loss, rejection, or discipline for the perpetrator. Sometimes the injustice is reality–based and would be upsetting to almost anyone. Other times the injustice seems to outside observers to have been blown significantly out of proportion.

Perpetrator: A violent individual, or one who presents an imminent danger.

Posing a threat: Implying through behavior or words that one intends to act violently.

Post Traumatic Stress Disorder (PTSD): A psychological syndrome that affects individuals who have been exposed to a traumatic event and who are experiencing intense fear, hopelessness, or horror. The symptoms must last more than 1 month and must significantly interfere with important areas of functioning (e.g., ability to work). The cluster of symptoms includes nightmares, flashbacks, hyperarousal, dissociation, depression, and avoidance.

Practice sessions: Lower level forms of violence conducted by schoolplace violence perpetrators and designed to "test out the system" and their own courage. These practice or rehearsal sessions can be engaged in either mentally, through violent fantasies, or physically, against lower level targets. Without intervention, practicing efforts can escalate from fantasy to violence. When practicing behaviors are noticed, protectors must work to create barriers to further escalation.

Primary victims: Those individuals who have experienced the violence directly. These are the people who are actually attacked or threatened during the assault.

Protectors: Those individuals or agencies that stand between potential perpetrators and their ability to commit violence. Protectors build insulation around possible victims not just when the shooting is occurring, but in the early stages of practice sessions and threats. There are formal protectors who are trained in their profession to de-escalate and interrupt violent situations. There are also informal protectors who rise to the occasion because they feel that it is the right thing to do, and because they have the skills and courage to do it.

Psychological profile: A behavioral analysis of individuals who have a propensity for violence. Traditional inductive methods of profiling looked at personality traits, innate temperament, violence characteristics, habits, and exposure to violence (real or dramatized) for the purposes of predicting future behavior. Current profiling technology is data-driven and is used on a case-by-case basis, relying on deductive methods. With this method, physical and behavioral evidence is gathered and synthesized to suggest possible future behavior as well as to help in assessing the risk of future violence.

PTSD: See Post Traumatic Stress Disorder.

Rampage or spree killers: Those who tend to kill as an act of passion and at a frantic pace. An example of a spree killer is Charles Whitman, the sniper who shot passersby from the tower at the University of Texas.

Reacting (as opposed to **Responding**): Usually involves a knee-jerk response to violence that is not predetermined and may put the person in greater danger.

Responding (as opposed to **Reacting**): Involves using a predetermined survival strategy against violence. There is less left to chance.

Schoolplace violence: An incident of violence that takes place on school grounds or during a school-related function in which a student retaliates against a perceived injustice, becomes an avenger, and uses deadly force against classmates, school staff, or law enforcement.

Secondary victims: The friends, witnesses, parents, rescue personnel, and others involved but not directly impacted by the violence. These secondary victims are often overlooked in trauma recovery efforts, but many of them may experience a post-traumatic response.

Shattered assumptions: A term developed by Dr. Ronnie Janoff-Bulman (1992) to describe what happens to people's assumptions about the world and humanity after they have experienced a trauma. When someone experiences a traumatic event, positive assumptions are thrown into question, and day-to-day functioning becomes a challenge.

Siege management kit: An emergency preparedness strategy that assembles blueprints of the school with exit routes clearly marked; important phone numbers; current school roster; information about main leads of water, gas, electricity, cable, and telephone; locations of alarm and sprinkler systems; and locations of hazardous materials and elevators—all for the purpose of notifying emergency responders. The efficacy of this kit depends on updating it on a regular basis.

Spree or rampage killers: See Rampage or spree killers.

Suicide-by-cop or **officer-assisted suicide:** Terms used when an individual decides to end his or her life by provoking the police into using deadly force.

Survivor guilt: A reaction some people have after experiencing a traumatic event whereby they blame themselves for what happened, often in an attempt to find some degree of control over an out-of-control situation.

Targeted violence: A term developed by the U.S. Secret Service to refer to any incident of violence where a known attacker selects a particular target prior to his or her violent attack. In the instances of school shootings, the target may be a classmate, a teacher, or the school building itself.

Tertiary victims: Helpers who also become affected by the violent event. These professionals may be dealing with their own reactions to the trauma or they may be vicariously affected by listening to story after story from the survivors. In some cases counselors may internalize another's pain and become overwhelmed. Their symptoms may in some cases resemble those of their clients.

Threat and Violence Assessment Team: Consists of individuals trained in the evaluation of and intervention with potentially violent situations.

TOADS: An acronym that stands for Time, Opportunity, Ability, Desire, and Stimulus. It is used to describe the factors that allow a person to become violent.

Trends: In this context, patterns of violence that alter the norms of our society. When threats and acts of violence are consistent over time, we adapt our way of living to minimize their impact. Our behavior changes. Soon, adjustment becomes second nature, and people do not consider the changes in behavior to be abnormal.

Triple overage. When someone is in charge of an important violence response function (e.g., notification of violence occurring), there should be two alternates as back up.

Veiled threats: Imply potential violence without directly stating the intent. They are vague and subject to interpretation. These types of threats are very real for the recipients, but may seem to lose some of their impact when repeated to others.

Victim of choice: The direct target of the assailant, the one against whom revenge is sought.

Victim of opportunity: An individual who happens to be in the vicinity when the violence occurs.

Village idiot effect: Occurs when the media seeks out an informant who is willing to give the press an inflammatory remark. If the media is bent on presenting a stereotype of the school, they will search for such an informant and additional harm will be done to the school's reputation. Therefore, each school should identify one spokesperson and an alternate to handle the press in the aftermath of a crisis.

Youth violence: A term broadly encapsulating all types of violence perpetrated by adolescents (the age span varies with different researchers).

Zero tolerance: In our proposal, not the familiar one–size–fits–all approach, but a policy aiming to deter violence by treating potential violence indicators seriously. Every threat gets addressed, even if that involves only investigation and documentation. Consequences for questionable behaviors and gestures should be appropriate to the level of severity the threat poses.

References

4 children stabbed at Alaska school. (2001, May 8). *The Washington Post*, p. A06.

34 things I learned from video games. (1995). Retrieved July 30, 2001, from http://www.cs.bgu.ac.il/~davidcha/Humor/learnedfromvideogames.html.

2000 Annual Report on School Safety. (2000). Washington DC: U.S. Department of Education & U.S. Department of Justice.

A public awakening—The Edmond post office massacre. (n.d.). Retrieved July 26, 1999, from http://www.svn.net/mikekell/v5.html.

Academic Universe Online. (2001). Gallup Poll (Question ID: US Gallup .01MH09, R30). Retrieved June 6, 2002, from http://web.lexis-nexis.com/universe/.

Adler, J., & Springen, K. (1999, May 3). How to fight back. *Newsweek*, 37.

Allen, J. (1998, April 3). Children should be held responsible for violence. *Oregon Daily Emerald*. Retrieved July 13, 1999, from http://www.darkwing.uoregon.edu/~ode/archieve/v99/3/980403/opin.html.

American Medical Association. (2001). School violence. Retrieved August 8, 2001, from www.ama-assn.org/ama/pub/article/2036-2512.html.

American Psychiatric Association. (2000). *Diagnostic and Statistical Manual of Mental Disorders* (4th ed., Text Revision). Washington, DC: Author.

Arnette, J., & Walsleben, M. (1998, April). Combating fear and restoring safety in schools. *Juvenile Justice Bulletin*. Washington, DC: U.S. Department of Justice.

Astor, A., Bahre, W., Fravil, K., & Wallace, J. (1997). Perception of school violence as a problem and reports of violent events: A national survey of school social workers. *Social Work, 42*(1), 55–69.

Atlas, R. S., & Pepler, D. J. (1998). Observations of bullying in the classroom. *Journal of Educational Research, 92*(2), 86.

Ballard, M., Argus, T., & Remley, T. (1999, May). Bullying and school violence: A proposed prevention program. *NASSP Bulletin, 83*(607), 38–47.

Best Practices of Youth Violence Prevention: A sourcebook for community action. (n.d.). National Center for Injury Prevention and Control. Retrieved August 8, 2001, from http://www.cdc.gov/ncipc/dvp/bestpractices.htm.

Brener, N., Simon, T., Krug, E., & Lowry, R. (1999). Recent trends in violence-related behaviors among high school students in the United States. *The Journal of the American Medical Association, 2829*(5), 440–446.

Bomb threats and physical security planning. (n.d.). Retrieved June 21, 2000, from http://nsi.org/Library/Terrorism/bombthreat.html.

Bower, A. (2001, March 19). Scorecard of hatred. *Time*, 30–31.

Caillouet, L. (1998). Bullets fly on campus: Fourth case in 6 months. *Arkansas Democrat-Gazette*. Retrieved July 13, 1999, from, http://www.ardemgaz.com/prev/jonesboro/acalls25.html.

Calif. school sued over weapons searches. (2001). Join Together Online. Retrieved August 1, 2001, from http://www.jointogether.org/gv/wire/news/reader.jtml?Object_ID=268002&PrintThis=true.

California Department of Education. (1998). *Early warning, timely response: A guide to safe schools*. Sacramento, CA: California Department of Education.

Center for the Study and Prevention of School Violence. (1999). *Stats 1999: Selected school violence research findings*. Retrieved June 5, 2001, from http://www.ncsu.edu/cpsv/eoto99.htm.

Center for the Study and Prevention of School Violence. (2000). *Stats 2000: Selected school violence research findings*. Retrieved July 25, 2001, from http://www.cpsv.org.

Center for the Study and Prevention of Violence. CSPV fact sheet: Student profiling. (1998a). Retrieved July 28, 2001, from http://www.colorado.edu/cspv/positions/position5.html.

Center for the Study and Prevention of Violence. (1998b). *Student Profiling: CSPV Position Summary*. Retrieved July 28, 2001, from http://www.colorado.edu/cspv/positions/position5.html.

Center for the Study and Prevention of Violence. CSPV fact sheet: Preventing firearm violence. (1999a). Retrieved July 28, 2001, from http://www.colorado.edu/cspv/factsheets/factsheet5.html.

Center for the Study and Prevention of Violence. CSPV fact sheet: School violence and social conditions. (1999b). Retrieved July 28, 2001, from http://www.colorado.edu/cspv/factsheets/factsheet6/html.

Center for the Study and Prevention of Violence. CSPV fact sheet: The youth violence problem. (1999c). Retrieved July 28, 2001, from http://www.colorado.edu/cspv/factsheets/factsheet16.html.

Center for the Study and Prevention of Violence. (2000). *Safe communities—Safe schools planning guide.* Boulder, CO: Author.

Center for the Study and Prevention of Violence. CSPV fact sheet: Responding to violence in the schools. (2001). Retrieved July 28, 2001, from http://www.colorado.edu/cspv/factsheets/Responding%20to%20Violence.htm.

Centers for Disease Control. (2000). Youth violence in the United States. Retrieved July 28, 2001, from http://www.cdc.gov/ncipc/factsheets/yvfacts.htm.

Centers for Disease Control. (2001). Facts about violence among youth and violence in schools. Retrieved July 28, 2001, from http://www.cdc.gov/ncipc/factsheets/schoolvi.htm.

Centers for Disease Control National Center for Injury Control and Prevention. (1996). *Ten leading causes of death, United States, 1996.* Atlanta, GA: U.S. Department of Health and Human Services, Centers for Disease Control.

Chandler, K., Chapman, C., Rand, M., & Taylor, B. (1998). *Students' reports of school crime: 1989 and 1995 (NCES Report 98-241).* Washington, DC: U.S. Departments of Education and Justice.

Chase, B. (1999, April). Learning bloody lessons: President's viewpoint. *NEA Today, 17*(7), 2.

Children say bullying, teasing big problems. (2001, March 8). Join Together Online. Retrieved May 10, 2001, from http://www.jointogether.org/gv/wire/news/reader.jtml?Object_ID=266313&PrintThis=true.

Cloud, J. (2001, March 19). The legacy of Columbine. *Time,* 32–35.

Colo. Law required bully-prevention policies. (2001, May 7). Join Together Online. Retrieved May 10, 2001, from http://www.jointogether.org/gv/news/reader.jtml?Object_ID=267439&PrintThis=true.

Columbine Review Commission. (2001). *The Report of Governor Bill Owens' Columbine Review Commission.* Denver, CO: State of Colorado.

Cottle, M. (1999, October 25). Workplace worrywarts. *New Republic, 221*(17), 11–12.

Crary, D. (2001, March 7). The bully factor: California shooting prompts new look at old problem. Associated Press Newswire.

Daniel, M. (2001, February 23). McDermott arraigned in Wakefield killings: Papers released detailing home, office searches. *The Boston Globe,* p. B2.

Dedman, B. (2000a, October 15). Bullying, tormenting often led to revenge in cases studied. *Chicago Sun-Times.* Retrieved June 5, 2001, from http://www.treas.gov/usss/ntac/chicago_sun/case15.htm.

Dedman, B. (2000b, October 15). Journals, poetry scream of violence, despair. *Chicago Sun-Times.* Retrieved July 25, 2001, from http://www.treas.gov/usss.ntac/chicago_sun/poem15.htm.

Dedman, B. (2000c, October 15). School shooters: Secret service findings. *Chicago Sun-Times.* Retrieved July 25, 2001, from http://www.trea.gove/usss/ntac/chicago_sun/find15.htm.

Dedman, B. (2000d, October 16). Schools may miss mark on preventing violence. *Chicago Sun-Times.* Retrieved July 25, 2001, from http://www.treas.gov/usss/ntac/chicago_sun/shoot16.htm.

Dedman, B. (2000e, October 16). Shooters usually tell friends what they are planning. *Chicago Sun-Times.* Retrieved July 25, 2001, from http://www.treas.gov/usss/chicago_sun/evan16.htm.

Donohue, E., Schiraldi, V., & Ziedenberg, J. (1998). Schoolhouse hype: School shootings and the real risks kids face in America. Retrieved August 8, 2001, from http://www.securitymanagement.com/library/schoolreport.html.

Dorfman, L. (2001). Off balance: Youth, race & crime in the news. Retrieved June 7, 2001, from http://www.buildingblocksforyouth.org/media/media.html.

Drugs, violence among top concerns of pre-teens. (2001, March 15). Join Together Online. Retrieved May 10, 2001, from http://www.jointogether.org/gv/wire/news/reader.jtml?Object_ID=266401&PrintThis=true.

Drug-using adolescents more likely to carry weapons. (2001, March 28). Join Together Online. Retrieved March 29, 2001, from http://www.jointogether.org/sa/news/summaries/print/0,1856,266547,00.html.

Eight young students stabbed to death in Japan. (2001). Join Together Online. Retrieved June 12, 2001, from http://www.jointogether.org/gv/wire/news/reader.jtml?Object_ID=267868&PrintThis=true.

Elliot, D. (1989). *National youth survey.* Ann Arbor, MI: Inter-university Consortium for Political and Social Research.

Elliot, D., Hamburg, B., & Williams, K. (1998). *Violence in American schools: A new perspective.* New York: Cambridge University Press.

Emergency Support Network, Australia. (n.d.). Critical incident support planning. Retrieved August 1, 2001, from http://207.174.231.85/ emergencysupport/art19.html.

Facing tragedy. (1999, April). *NEA Today, 17*(7), 6.

The facts about school violence. (2000). The Trustees of Indiana University. Retrieved July 25, 2001, from http://www.indiana.edu/~safeschl/facts.html.

Federal Bureau of Investigation. (1998). *Uniform crime reports for the United States, 1996.* Washington, DC: U.S. Department of Justice.

Fein, R., & Vossekuil, B. (1995, July). Threat assessment: An approach to prevent targeted violence. *National Institute of Justice: Research in Action.* Washington, DC: U.S. Department of Justice.

Ferguson, H. (2001, May). Looking beyond the school shooter profile: Developing a comprehensive protocol for school violence prevention. *The Police Chief,* 48–52.

Fessenden, F. (2000, April 9). Profiles of 102 rampage killers show mental illness warnings. *Denver Rocky Mountain News,* pp. 2A, 64A, 67A, 69A.

Fey, G., Nelson, J., & Roberts, M. (2000, February). The perils of profiling. *The School Administrator,* 12–16.

Five charged in Texas shooting plot. (1998). Associated Press. Retrieved April 24, 1999 from the AOL News database.

Foo, R., & Vasquez, D. (2001, January 31). *Ventura County Star,* p. A01. Photo lab's tip foils bomb plot: Teen allegedly planned mass killings at college.

Gibbs, N. (1999, May 3). Special report: The Littleton massacre. *Time, 29.*

Gibbs, N., & Roche, T. (1999, December 20). The Columbine tapes. *Time,* 40–51.

Goldberg, M. (1997). News flash: Mom says Pearl Jam video upset son accused of killing three. Retrieved July 13, 1999, from http://www.addict.com/MNOTW/lofi/970911/970911_1176.shtml.

Gottfredson, D. (1998). School-based crime prevention. In L. Sherman, D. Gottfreson, D. MacKenzie, J. Eck, P. Ruter, & S. Bushway (Eds.), *Preventing crime: What works, what doesn't, what's promising: A report to the United States Congress* (1–74). Washington, DC: U.S. Department of Justice, Office of Justice Programs.

Gottfredson, D., Fink, C., Skroban, S., & Gottfredson, G. (1997). Making prevention work. *Establishing Preventive Services. Healthy Children 2010. Issues in Children's and Families' Lives, Vol. 9,* PS 026 124.

Gottfredson, G., Gottsfredson, D., Czeh, E., Cantor, Crosse, & Hantman. (2000). *Summary: National study of delinquency prevention in schools.* Ellicott City, MD: Gottfredson Associates.

Groves, M., & Krikorian, M. (2001, March 8). Arrests reflect fear of more school violence. *Los Angeles Times*, p. 1.

Guns in American schools. (1998). Retrieved July 13, 1999, from http://www.handguncontrol.org/protecting/D1/d1gunsch.htm.

Gutloff, K. (1999, April). Safe schools. *NEA Today*, 17(7), 4–5.

Harpold, J. (1998, October). *Lessons learned: An FBI perspective gleaned from six police jurisdictions experiencing school violence.* Paper presented at the National Conference on Preventing Crime, Washington, DC.

Hall, C. (1998, December 6). Our schools' lost innocence: Is violent pop culture holding kids hostage? *The Courier-Journal.* Retrieved July 13, 1999, from http://www.courier-journal.com/cjextra/schoolshoot/SCHpopculture.html.

Headden, S., & Kulman, L. (1997, July 28). A search for clues to a killer's spree. *U.S. News.* Retrieved August 8, 2001, from http://www.usnews.com/usnews/issue/980828/28kill.htm.

Heaviside, S., Rowand, C., Williams, C., & Farris, E. (1998). *Violence and discipline problems in U.S. Public Schools: 1996–97 (NCES 98-030).* Washington, DC: U.S. Department of Education, National Center for Education Statistics.

Herman, J. (1992). *Trauma and recovery: The aftermath of violence—from domestic abuse to political terror.* Scranton, PA: HarperCollins.

Hughes, J. (1996). Television violence: Implications for violence prevention. *The School Psychology Review*, 25(2), 134–151.

International Association of Chiefs of Police. (2001). *Guide for Preventing and Responding to School Violence.* Alexandria, VA: Author.

Janoff-Bulman, R. (1992). *Shattered assumptions: Toward a new psychology of trauma.* New York: The Free Press.

Jonesboro shooting. (1999). Associated Press. Retrieved July 13, 1999, from http://www.usatoday.com/news/special/shoot/shoot0004.htm.

Kennish, J. (n.d.). Preparing for bomb threats. Retrieved June 21, 2000, from http://www.kennish.com/bombthreat.

Kenworthy, T., & O'Driscoll, P. (2000, April 14). Columbine changes schools' inner world. *USA Today.* Retrieved May 18, 2000, from http://www.usatoday.com/news/index/colo/colo192.htm.

Kinkel's friends ignored warning signs: Parents tried to deal with son's discipline problems. (1998). Associated Press. Retrieved July 13, 1999, from http://www.channel6000.com/news/stories/news-980422-193816.html.

Knox, M., Carey, M., Kim, W., & Niedermeier, D. (2000, August). Relationships among violence exposure, depression, and aggressive behavior in youth. Paper presented at the Annual Conference of the American Psychological Association, Washington, DC.

Law enforcement discover plot at high school. (2001, February 5). The Associated Press State and Local Wire.

Lefevre, G. (1998, May 23). Profile of high school shooting suspect. Retrieved July 13, 1999, from http://www.cnnsf.com/newsvault/output/spring.html.

Lester, W. (2001, March 14). Teens fear more school shootings. The Detroit News, Two Dot; Issue: PSA–2805; Front Section.

Loeber, R., & Farrington, D. (1998). *Serious and violent juvenile offenders: Risk factors and successful interventions.* Thousand Oaks, CA: Sage.

Lofholm, N. (1998, July 16). Deadly school violence targeted Attorneys General to tackle issue. *Denver Post*, p. B04.

MacDonald, J., Shaughnessy, R., & Galvin, J. (1977). Bomb threats. In *Bombers & Firesetters*, Springfield, IL; Charles C. Thomas.

Many Colo. students afraid of bullies. (2000, November 20). Join Together Online. Retrieved May 10, 2001, from http://www.jointogether.org/gv/wire/news/reader.jtml?Object_ID=265146&PrintThis=true.

Martin, R. (2001). American Bar Association zero tolerance report. Retrieved July 30, 2001, from http://www.abanet.org/scripts/PrintView.asp.

McCarthy, T. (2001, March 19). Warning: Andy Williams here. *Time*, 24–28.

McGee, J., & DeBernardo, C. (n.d.). *Classroom avenger profile.* Sheppard and Enoch Pratt Health System, P.O. Box 6815, Baltimore, MD 21285. Unpublished manuscript.

McGibbon, G. (1999, June 13). Columbine: Looking for answers. *The Denver Post*, 27A, 29A.

Mediascope. (n.d.). *Media violence and children.* Retrieved August 15, 1999, from http://www.mediascope.org/mediascope/medvioch.htm.

Mercy, J., & Rosenberg, M. (1998). Preventing firearm violence in and around schools. In D. Elliot, B. Hamburg, & K. Williams (Eds.), *Violence in American schools: A new perspective*, (159–197). New York: NY: Cambridge University Press.

Miniclier, K., & Robinson, M. (1999, May 8). Officials find plans for an attack, along with a map of Adams City High School. *The Denver Post*, p. B-01.

Mitchell, K. (n.d.). Shooting hits home for firefighter. Retrieved July 26, 1999, from http://www.denverpost.com/news/gre1209a.htm.

Motive not known for attack on Alaska elementary students. (2001, May 7). Retrieved June 20, 2001, from http://www.cnn.com/2001/US/05/07/alaska.school.stabbing.02/index.html.

Mountain States Employers Council & Nicoletti-Flater Associates. (1997). *Violence goes to work: An employer's guide.* Denver, CO: Authors.

National Education Association. (1999, March 29). On school shooting anniversaries, *NEA Today* brings focus to school safety. Press release. Retrieved July 13, 1999, from http://www.nea.org/nr/nr990329.html.

National Institute on Media and the Family. (1999). *Effects of video game playing on children.* Retrieved May 26, 1999, from http://www.mediaandthefamily.com/effect.html.

National PTA. (1999). 10 things you can do. Retrieved July 17, 2001, from http://www.pta.org/programs/crisis/10/do1.htm.

National School Boards Association. (1999, August 9). Keep schools safe. Retrieved August 15, 1999, from http://www.nsba.org/.

National School Safety Center. (1999). America's safe schools week. Retrieved August 10, 1999, from http://www.nsscl.org/safeweek/safe.htm.

National School Safety Center. (2001). School-associated violent deaths. Retrieved May 16, 2001, from http://www.nsscl.org.

Nicoletti, J., Spencer-Thomas, S., & Porter, K. (1998). *Survival-oriented kids in a violent world: A skills training manual for parents and other protectors.* Lakewood, CO: Nicoletti-Flater Associates.

Nicoletti, J., Spencer-Thomas, S., & Bollinger, C. (2001). *Violence goes to college: The authoritative guide to prevention and intervention.* Springfield, IL: Charles C. Thomas.

Pankratz, H. (2000, July 27). Virtual realities spur school massacres, Das told. *The Denver Post,* p. A15.

Phillips, P. (1999, May 15). Police foil Michigan school shooting plans. USA TV Talk. Retrieved July 13, 1999, from http://www.bruhmedia.net/rhsmessages/27.html.

Pittel, E. (1998). How to take a weapons history: Interviewing children at risk for violence at school. *American Academy of Child and Adolescent Psychiatry, 37*(10), 1100–1102.

Pitts, L. (2000, May 11). In these times, student's words ring alarm. *Denver Post*, p. B11.

Portrait of a high school killer. (1999, April 28). CBS Worldwide Corp. Retrieved July 13, 1999, from http://www.cbs.com/flat/story_148134.html.

Post office finally realizes it may have a violence problem (1998). Retrieved July 26, 1999, from http://www.wco.com.

Prendergast, A. (1999, August 5–11). Doom rules: Much of what we think we know about Columbine is wrong. *Westword*, 22(49), 22–35.

Preventing school violence. (n.d.). Join Together Online. Retrieved May 10, 2001, from http://www.jointogether.org/gv/resource.../reader.jtml?Tab=&Object_ID =267470&PrintThis=true.

Prial, E. (1999). Death at the hand of police: Suicide or homicide? Paper presented at the Conference on Suicide and Law Enforcement at the Behavioral Science Unit of the FBI Academy; Quantico, VA, September 21–23, 1999.

Pritchett, J. (1999, April 29). "Freaky" Marilyn Manson fan lived his life on the Internet: Nobody liked him, everyone ridiculed him. *The Ottawa Citizen*, p. A1.

Rambling intruder stabs 4 kids at Alaska school (2001, May 8). *The Record of Northern New Jersey*, p. 336.

Randall, K. (2001, February 10). Another workplace shooting in the U.S.: Five dead at Chicago Navistar plant. Retrieved June 20, 2001, from http://wsws.org/ articles/2001/feb2001/shot-f10.shtml.

Robinson, M., & Chronis, P. (1999, May 15). High school freshman held in Columbine copycat plot. *The Denver Post.* p. B–03.

Rodriguez, A., Yates, J., & Marx, G. (2001, February 6). Convicted ex–worker kills 5 in Melrose Park. *Chicago Tribune.* Retrieved June 20, 2001, from http:// chicagotribune.com/news/printedition/article/0,2669,SAV–0102060231,FF.html.

Rouse claims he was "mouthing off" about killing teachers. (1998, March 30). Retrieved July 13, 1999, from www.oakridger.com/stories/033098/ aps_rouse.html.

Safe & Responsive Schools Project. (2000a). Effective responses. Indiana University Education Policy Center. Retrieved July 25, 2001, from http://www.indiana.edu/ ~safeschl/response.html.

Safe & Responsive Schools Project. (2000b). Zero tolerance. Indiana University Education Policy Center. Retrieved July 25, 2001, from http://www.indiana.edu/ ~safeschl/zero.html.

Satore Township. (1999). *An obsession with Laura.* Retrieved July 26, 1999, from http://www.svn.net/mikekell/farley.html.

School shooting threats disrupt learning. (2001, May 30). Join Together Online. Retrieved May 31, 2001, from http://www.jointogether.org/gv/wire/news/ reader.jtml?Object_ID=267751&PrintThis=true.

School suspension over violent poem deemed appropriate. (2001). Join Together Online. Retrieved August 1, 2001, from http://www.jointogether.org/gv/wire/ news/reader.jtml?Object_ID=554940&PrintThis=true.

Schoolyard killers. (1998, November 7). *Cincinnati Post.* Retrieved July 13, 1999, from http://www.cincypost.com/news/listk110798.html.

Security Resource Net. (n.d.). Retrieved June 21, 2000, from http://nsi.org/library/ terrorism/bombthreat.html.

Shooting occurred despite Santana's prevention efforts. (2001, March 9). Join Together Online. Retrieved May 10, 2001, from http://www.jointogether.org/ gv/wire/news/reader.jtml?Object_ID=266327&PrintThis=true.

Shooting suspect boasted of violence: Friend says Kinkel was angry at parents for being grounded. (1998). Associated Press. Retrieved July 13, 1999, from www.channel6000.com/news/stories/news-980521-203250.html.

Simpson, K. (1999, December 15). Killers' rampage plan banked on media frenzy. *The Denver Post,* p. A17.

Skiba, R. (2000). *Zero tolerance, zero evidence: An analysis of school disciplinary practice.* Bloomington, IN: Indiana Education Policy Center.

Slover, C., & Tasci, T. (1999). *Trauma recovery handbook.* Lakewood, CO: Nicoletti– Flater Associates.

Snyder, H., & Sickmund, M. (1995). *Juvenile offenders and victims: A national report.* Washington, DC: Office of Juvenile Justice and Delinquency Prevention.

Some Americans fear school shootings in their community. (2001, April 24). *USA Today,* p. 01A.

Spivak, H., & Prothrow–Stith, D. (2001). The need to address bullying—An important component of violence prevention. *The Journal of the American Medical Association, 285*(16), 2131–2133.

Stats 1999: Selected school violence research findings. (n.d.). Center for the Prevention of School Violence. Retrieved June 5, 2001, from http:// www.ncsu.edu/cpsv/eoto99.htm.

Stats 2000: Selected school violence research findings. (n.d.). Center for the Prevention of School Violence. Retrieved July 25, 2001, from http://www.cpsv.org.

Stephens, R. (1995). *Safe schools: A handbook for violence prevention.* Bloomington, IN: National Educational Service.

Student dies after Calgary school stabbing. (2000, November 21). CBC News. Retrieved June 20, 2001, from http://cbc.ca/cgi-bin/templates/Nwview.cgi?/news/2000/11/20/stabbing_001120.

Survey shows students have easy access to guns. (2001, April 3). Join Together Online. Retrieved May 10, 2001, from http://www.jointogether.org/gv/wire/news/reader.jtml?Object_ID=266992&PrintThis=true.

Teen charged in Calgary school stabbing. (2000, November 21). Retrieved June 20, 2001, from http://toronto.globaltv.com/ca/news/stories/news-20001121-094451.html.

Threats mount in schools: More violent statements reported. (1998). Associated Press. Retrieved July 13, 1999, from http://www.channel6000.com/news/stories/news-980527-083931.html.

Traumatic events: Is there a danger of over reaction?. (n.d.). Retrieved August 1, 2001, from http://207.174.231.85/emergencysupport/art8.html.

Trench-coated gunmen in Colorado bring memories of Loukaitis. (1999). Retrieved July 13, 1999, from http://www.seattleinsider.com/news/1999/04/20/loukaitis.html.

Trompetter, P. (1999a, September). School shootings: Implications for "Suicide-by-cop." Paper presented at the Conference on Suicide and Law Enforcement at the Behavioral Science Unit of the FBI Academy; Quantico, VA.

Trompetter, P. (1999b). *School shootings: Vignettes and commonalities.* Unpublished manuscript.

Two students arrested for allegedly plotting killings. (1999, August 25). The Associated Press State & Local Wire.

U.S. Department of Education. (2000). Indicators of school crime and safety: 2000. National Center for educational Statistics and Bureau of Justice Statistics. Retrieved June 5, 2001, from http://nces.ed.gov/pubs2001/quarterly/winter/elementary/e_section4.html.

U.S. Secret Service National Threat Assessment Center. (2000). *Safe school initiative: An interim report on the prevention of targeted violence in schools.* Washington, DC: Department of the Treasury.

U.S. Surgeon General. (2001a). Fact sheet–at a glance: Messages. Retrieved July 28, 2001, from http://www.surgeongeneral.gov/library/youthviolence/messages.htm.

U.S. Surgeon General. (2001b). *Youth violence: A report of the Surgeon General.* Rockville, MD: Office of the Surgeon General. Retrieved July 28, 2001, from http://www.surgeongenral.gov/library/youthvioence/default.htm.

The Virtual Office of the Surgeon General. (2001). Fact sheet—At a glance: Messages. Retrieved July 28, 2001, from http://www.surgeongeneral.gov/library/youthviolence/messages.htm.

Walker, T. (1999, November 10). *The Denver Post*, p. F-03. Steven King asks for an end to "Rage."

Workplace tension, monotony may have set off gunman, postal workers say. (1997). Retrieved July 26, 1999, from http://www.news-star.com/122097/new_postal.html.

Wright, J., & Hartman, J. (1998, May 28). Suspect's dad sought National Guard help. *The Register-Guard*, p. 4A.

Yingst, C. (n.d.). Past killings expose crisis in Redlands. Retrieved July 13, 1999, from http://www.dadi.org/KidKill2.htm.

Zuckoff, M. (1999, May 21). Georgia school shooting. *Boston Globe*, p. A1.

Additional Resources

The following list of resources is not exhaustive, but is intended to give readers assistance in developing and enhancing comprehensive school safety plans. Many of these resources complement the material presented in this book by giving more thorough suggestions for long–term prevention and trauma recovery.

Violence Prevention and Intervention

American Psychological Association. (1993). *Violence and youth: Psychology's response (Vol. 1)*. Washington, DC: Author.

Baron, S. (1993). *Violence in the workplace*. Ventura, CA: Pathfinder.

By Kids 4 Kids. (n.d.). *Not my friends–Not my school*. Video. Eugene, OR: Chambers Communication. Made available from http://www.ribbonof promise.org.

The Creative Partnership for Prevention (http://www.cpprev.org), sponsored by the U.S. Department of Education's Safe and Drug–Free Schools Program.

Drug Strategies (Ed.). (1998). *Safe schools, safe students: A guide to violence prevention strategies*. Washington, DC: Author.

Dwyer, K., Osher, D., & Warger, C. (1998). *Early warning, timely response: A guide to safe schools*. Washington, DC: U.S. Department of Education.

Elliot, D., Hamburg, B., & Williams, K. (1998). *Violence in American schools: A new perspective*, New York: Cambridge University Press.

Eron, L. D., Gentry, J. H., & Schlegel, P. (Eds.). (1994). *Reason to hope: A psychological perspective on violence and youth*. Washington, DC: American Psychological Association.

Furlong, M. J., & Smith, D. C. (Eds.). (1994). *Anger, hostility, and aggression: Assessment, prevention, and intervention strategies for youth*. Brandon, VT: Clinical Psychology.

Guerra, N., & Tolan, P. (1994). *What works in reducing adolescent violence: An empirical review of the field (Rep. No. F-888)*. Boulder, CO: University of Colorado, Center for the Study and Prevention of Violence.

Hipp, E. (2000). *Understanding the human volcano: What teens can do about violence.* Center City, MN: Hazelden.

Join Together Online–http://www.jointogether.org.

Kellerman, J. (1999). *Savage spawn: Reflections on violent children.* New York: Library of Contemporary Thought, Valentine.

Kinney, J., & Johnson, D. L. (1993). *Breaking point: The workplace violence epidemic and what to do about it.* Chicago: National Safe Workplace Institute.

Langone, J. (1984). *Violence: Our fastest growing public health problem.* Boston-Toronto: Little, Brown.

Mahaffy, R. (Ed.). (1995). *Safe schools: A handbook for practitioners.* Reston, VA: National Association of Secondary School Principals.

National Association of School Psychologists–http://www.naspweb.org.

National Crime Prevention Council Fulfillment Center
P.O. Box 1
100 Church Street
Amsterdam, NY 12010
Tel: 800-NCPC-911
Fax: 518-843-6857

National Mental Health and Education Center. (2000, Winter). *Behavioral interventions: Creating a safe environment in our schools.* Bethesda, MD: National Association of School Psychologists.

National PTA–http://www.pta.org

National Resource Center for Safe Schools–http://www.safetyzone.org

National School Safety Center–http://www.nssc1.org

Prevention Online (PREVLINE)–http://www.health.org. A national clearinghouse sponsored by the Substance Abuse and Mental Health Services Administration.

Ribbon of Promise–http://www.ribbonofpromise.org. Campaign organized after the massacre at Thurston High School in Springfield, Oregon.

Safe and Drug-Free Schools Program–http://www.ed.gov/offices/OESE/SDFS.

Shure, M. B. (1996). *Raising a thinking child: Help your young child to resolve everyday conflicts and get along with others: The 'I can problem solve' program.* Riverside, NJ: Pocket Books.

Shure, M. B. (2000). *Raising a thinking child workbook: Teaching young children to resolve everyday conflicts and get along with others.* Champaign, IL: Research Press.

Shure, M. B. (2001). *Raising a thinking preteen: The 'I can problem solve' program for 8- to 12-year-olds.* New York: Henry Holt.

U. S. Department of Health and Human Services. (1993). *Request for assistance in preventing homicide in the workplace.* Cincinnati, OH: NIOSH Alert.

VandenBos, G. R., & Bulatao, E. Q. (Eds.). (1996). *Violence on the job: Identifying risks and developing solutions.* Washington, DC: American Psychological Association.

Weltmann, R., & Huml, F. J. (Eds.). (1998). *Ready-to-use violence prevention skills: Lessons & activities for secondary students.* New York: Prentice Hall.

Youth Violence and Suicide Prevention Team, National Center for Injury Prevention and Control–http://www.cdc.gov/ncipc/dvp/yvpt/yvpt.htm. An informational site supported by the Centers for Disease Control.

Violence Aftermath

Project SERV (School Emergency Response to Violence)–Grant to help schools respond to crisis needs including increased security and counseling. Funded by the U.S. Department of Education. For more information call (202) 260-1862.

Trauma Recovery (Adult)

Herman, J. L. (1997). *Trauma and recovery.* New York: Basic Books.

Janoff–Bulman, R. (1992). *Shattered assumptions: Towards a new psychology of trauma.* New York: The Free Press.

Levine, P. A. (1997). *Waking the tiger: Healing trauma.* Berkeley, CA: North Atlantic Books.

Matsakis, A. (1992). *I can't get over it: A handbook for trauma survivors.* Oakland, CA: New Harbinger.

McCann, I. L., & Pearlman, L. A. (1990). *Psychological trauma and the adult survivor: Theory, therapy, and transformation.* New York: Brunner/Mazel.

Parkinson, F. (1993). *Post-trauma stress: A personal guide to reduce the long-term effect and hidden emotional damage caused by violence and disaster.* Tucson, AZ: Fisher Books.

Slover, C., & Tasci, D. (1999). *Trauma recovery handbook.* Denver, CO: Nicoletti–Flater Associates.

Viorst, J. (1998). *Necessary losses: The loves, illusions, dependencies and impossible expectations that all of us have to give up in order to grow.* New York: Simon & Schuster.

Trauma Recovery (Child)

Deskin, G., & Steckler, G. (1996). *When nothing makes sense: Disaster, crisis and their effects on children.* Minneapolis, MN: Fairview Press.

Johnson, K. (1998). *Trauma in the lives of children: Crisis and stress management techniques for counselors, teachers, and other professionals.* Alameda, CA: Hunter House.

Monahan, C. (1993). *Children and trauma: A parent's guide to helping children heal.* New York: Lexington Books.

Monahan, C. (1997). *Children and trauma: A guide for parents and professionals.* Somerset, NJ: Jossey–Bass.

Schaefer, D., & Lyons, C. (1993). *How do we tell the children?: A step-by-step guide for helping children two to teen cope when someone dies.* New York: Newmarket Press.

Terr, L. (1990). *Too scared to cry: Psychic trauma in childhood.* New York: Harper and Row.

Debriefing

Mitchell, J. T., & Everly, G. (1995). *Critical incident stress debriefing: An operations manual for the prevention of traumatic stress among emergency services and disaster workers (2nd Ed).* Ellicott City, MD: Chevron.

Emergency Support Network–http://207.174.231.85/emergencysupport. A training organization in Western Australia.

Index

About *Violence Goes to School* and the National Educational Service

The mission of the National Educational Service is to provide tested and proven resources that help those who work with youth create safe and caring schools, agencies, and communities where all children succeed. *Violence Goes to School* is just one of many resources and staff development opportunities NES provides that focuses on building a community circle of caring. If you have any questions, comments, or manuscripts you would like us to consider for publication, please contact us at the address below or visit our Web site at:

www.nesonline.com

Staff Development Opportunities Include:

Bullying Prevention
Effective Parenting
Creating Professional Learning Communities
Building Cultural Bridges
Discipline With Dignity
Ensuring Safe Schools
Managing Disruptive Behavior
Reclaiming Youth at Risk
Teaching Self Control

National Educational Service
304 W. Kirkwood Avenue, Suite 2
Bloomington, IN 47404-5132
(812) 336-7700
(800) 733-6786 (toll-free number)
FAX (812) 336-7790
e-mail: nes@nesonline.com
www.nesonline.com

NEED MORE COPIES OR ADDITIONAL RESOURCES ON THIS TOPIC?

Need more copies of this book? Want your own copy? Need additional resources on this topic? If so, you can order additional materials by using this form or by calling us toll free at (800) 733-6786 or (812) 336-7700. Or you can order by FAX at (812) 336-7790, or visit our Web site at www.nesonline.com.

Title	Price*	Quantity	Total
Teasing and Harassment: The Frames and Scripts Approach for Teachers and Parents	$ 9.95		
Anger Management for Youth	24.95		
As Tough As Necessary: Discipline With Dignity (video)	395.00		
Discipline with Dignity for Challenging Youth	24.95		
Discipline with Dignity (video)	356.00		
Parents Assuring Student Success	24.95		
Power Struggles	11.95		
Set Straight on Bullies (video)	139.00		
Teaching Self-Control	27.95		
The Bullying Prevention Handbook	23.95		
		SUBTOTAL	
		SHIPPING	
Continental U.S.: Please add 6% of order total. Outside continental U.S.: Please add 8% of order total.			
		HANDLING	
Continental U.S.: Please add $4. Outside continental U.S.: Please add $6.			
		TOTAL (U.S. funds)	

*Price subject to change without notice.

❏ Check enclosed   ❏ Purchase order enclosed
❏ Money order   ❏ VISA, MasterCard, Discover, or American Express (circle one)

Credit Card No._____ Exp. Date_____
Cardholder Signature _____

SHIP TO:

First Name_____ Last Name_____
Position _____
Institution Name_____
Address_____
City_____ State_____ ZIP_____
Phone_____ FAX_____
E-mail _____

National Educational Service
304 W. Kirkwood Avenue, Suite 2
Bloomington, IN 47404-5132
(812) 336-7700 • (800) 733-6786 (toll-free number)
FAX (812) 336-7790
e-mail: nes@nesonline.com • www.nesonline.com